Ten Twentieth-Century Indian Poets

Chosen and Edited by
R. PARTHASARATHY

DELHI
OXFORD UNIVERSITY PRESS
LONDON NEW YORK MELBOURNE
1976

Oxford University Press

OXFORD LONDON GLASGOW NEW YORK
TORONTO MELBOURNE WELLINGTON CAPE TOWN
IBADAN NAIROBI DAR ES SALAAM LUSAKA ADDIS ABABA
KUALA LUMPUR SINGAPORE JAKARTA HONG KONG TOKYO
DELHI BOMBAY CALCUTTA MADRAS KARACHI

Printed in India by P. K. Ghosh
at Eastend Printers, 3 Dr Suresh Sarkar Road, Calcutta 700 014
and published by R. Dayal, Oxford University Press,
2/11 Ansari Road, Daryaganj, New Delhi 110 002

Ten Twentieth-Century
Indian Poets

THREE CROWNS BOOKS

Poetry
Keki N. Daruwalla: *Crossing of Rivers*
Nissim Ezekiel: *Hymns in Darkness*
Shiv K. Kumar: *Subterfuges*
Oswald Mbuyiseni Mtshali: *Sounds of a Cowhide Drum*
Kaleem Omar (ed.): *Wordfall*
R. Parthasarathy: *Rough Passage*
R. Parthasarathy (ed.): *Ten Twentieth-Century Indian Poets*
A. K. Ramanujan: *Selected Poems*

Drama
J. P. Clark: *Ozidi*
J. P. Clark: *Three Plays*
Gurcharan Das: *Larins Sahib*
R. Sarif Easmon: *Dear Parent and Ogre*
Obi B. Egbuna: *The Anthill*
Athol Fugard: *Boesman and Lena*
Athol Fugard: *Hello and Goodbye*
Athol Fugard: *People are Living There*
Tsegaye Gabre-Medhin: *Oda Oak Oracle*
J. C. de Graft: *Sons and Daughters*
J. C. de Graft: *Through a Film Darkly*
Tewfik al-Hakim: *The Tree Climber*
Girish Karnad: *Hayavadana*
Howard McNaughton (ed.): *Contemporary New Zealand Plays*
Sonny Oti: *The Old Masters*
Ola Rotimi: *The Gods are not to Blame*
Ola Rotimi: *Kurunmi*
Ola Rotimi: *Our Husband's Gone Mad Again*
Ola Rotimi: *Ovonramwen Nogbaisi*
Badal Sircar: *Evam Indrajit*
Wole Soyinka: *A Dance of the Forests*
Wole Soyinka: *Kongi's Harvest*
Wole Soyinka: *The Lion and the Jewel*
Wole Soyinka: *The Road*
Wole Soyinka: *Three Short Plays*
Joris Wartemburg: *The Corpse's Comedy*

Fiction
U. R. Anantha Murthy: *Samskara*
Obi B. Egbuna: *Daughters of the Sun and Other Stories*
Barbara Kimenye: *Kalasanda*
Barbara Kimenye: *Kalasanda Revisited*
David Umobuarie: *Black Justice*

Non-fiction
Arnold Apple: *Son of Guyana*

For
LANCELOT RIBEIRO
DONN P. BYRNE

Contents

Preface

I should like to thank all the poets in this book for their kindness in allowing me to reprint from their published works and to look over their unpublished manuscripts. Their generosity has made this book possible. My thanks are due to the publishers and the editors of the periodicals, where some of the poems first appeared, for permission to reprint.

It has been a great pleasure to discuss this book in the making with friends, and I am indebted to Nissim Ezekiel, Roger Iredale, S. Krishnan, Shiv K. Kumar, Jayanta Mahapatra, C. D. Narasimhaiah, K. Ayyappa Paniker, A. K. Ramanujan and M. Sivaram Krishna for reading the book in manuscript, offering suggestions and for their continuing help and co-operation.

R. PARTHASARATHY

Madras, February 1976

Acknowledgements

The editor and publishers gratefully acknowledge permission to reproduce copyright poems in this book.

KEKI N. DARUWALLA

For 'The Epileptic 1', 'The Ghaghra in Spate' and 'Ruminations 1' from *Under Orion*, published by Writers Workshop, to the author and the publishers. For 'Fire-hymn' and 'Routine' from *Apparition in April*, published by Writers Workshop, to the author and the publishers. For 'Death of a Bird' from *Crossing of Rivers*, published by Oxford University Press, to the author and the publishers.

KAMALA DAS

For 'The Freaks', 'My Grandmother's House', 'A Hot Noon in Malabar' and 'The Sunshine Cat' from *Summer in Calcutta*, published by Rajinder Paul, to the author and the publishers. For 'The Invitation' and 'The Looking-glass' from *The Descendants*, published by Writers Workshop, to the author and the publishers.

NISSIM EZEKIEL

For 'Enterprise' from *The Unfinished Man*, published by Writers Workshop, to the author and the publishers. For 'Philosophy', 'Night of the Scorpion', 'Poet, Lover, Birdwatcher' and 'The Visitor' from *The Exact Name*, published by Writers Workshop, to the author and the publishers. For 'Background, Casually', 'Goodbye Party for Miss Pushpa T. S.' and 'Poem of the Separation' from *Hymns in Darkness*, published by Oxford University Press, to the author and the publishers.

ARUN KOLATKAR

For 'the boatride', to the author and *damn you*. For 'Jejuri', to the author and *Opinion Literary Quarterly*.

SHIV K. KUMAR

For 'Indian Women', 'My Co-respondent' and 'Pilgrimage' from *Cobwebs in the Sun*, published by Tata McGraw-Hill Publishing Co. Ltd., to the author and the publishers. For 'Days in New York' and 'Kali' from *Subterfuges*, published by Oxford University Press, to the author and the publishers.

JAYANTA MAHAPATRA

For 'Indian Summer', 'A Missing Person' and 'The Whorehouse in a Calcutta Street' from *A Rain of Rites*, published by the University of Georgia Press, to the author and the publishers. For 'The Logic' from *Indian Poetry in English Today*, published by Sterling Publishers Ltd., to the author and the publishers. For 'Grass' and 'Lost', published here for the first time, to the author.

ARVIND KRISHNA MEHROTRA

For 'The Sale', to the author and *The New York Quarterly*. For 'Continuities', to the author and *Modern Poetry in Translation*. For 'A Letter to a Friend', to the author and *The American Review*. For 'Remarks of an Early Biographer', published here for the first time, to the author.

R. PARTHASARATHY

For 'Exile 2, 8', 'Trial 1, 2, 7, 9, 10' and 'Homecoming 1, 3, 4, 8, 10, 12, 14' from *Rough Passage*, published by Oxford University Press, to the author and the publishers.

GIEVE PATEL

For 'On Killing a Tree', 'Servants', 'Nargol' and 'Naryal Purnima' from *Poems*, published by Nissim Ezekiel, to the author and the publishers. For 'Commerce', to the author and *Mahfil*. For 'O My Very Own Cadaver', published here for the first time, to the author.

A. K. RAMANUJAN

For 'Looking for a Cousin on a Swing' and 'A River' from *The Striders*, published by Oxford University Press, to the author and the publishers. For 'Of Mothers, among Other Things', 'Love Poem for a Wife 1', 'Small-scale Reflections on a Great House' and 'Obituary' from *Relations*, published by Oxford University Press, to the author and the publishers.

Introduction

1

In the mid-fifties *Quest,* the influential bimonthly of arts and ideas then edited by Nissim Ezekiel, did much to encourage a whole generation of poets, a task to which it devoted itself again in 1972 when it offered its pages to an assessment of the recent poetic scene, and provided thereby a platform for both new and established poets. In the present selection, however, only ten poets are included as a sample of what I consider significant in twentieth-century Indian verse in English. I would like to believe that the choices also broadly reflect the consensus of readers today who take Indian verse in English seriously. My loyalty has throughout been to poems rather than to reputations.

2

It is nearly one hundred and fifty years since Indian poets gathered under the common umbrella of the English language. The earliest attempt, as far as I know, to present them in a book was undertaken at the instance of E. V. Rieu, and published by Oxford University Press in 1920. This was *India in Song: Eastern Themes in English Verse by British and Indian Poets.* Introducing the anthology, the editor, Theodore Douglas Dunn, Inspector of Schools, Presidency Division, Bengal, wrote:

The period to which the verse of this collection belongs is roughly the century beginning about the year 1817; and the authors represented are both Indian and English. It is not generally known that during this century much good English verse was produced by Indians . . .

It is unlikely that the present generation will endorse Dunn's opinion. Only Toru Dutt had talent, and even she is chiefly remembered for one, unique poem, 'Our Casuarina Tree'. Henry Derozio's *Poems* (1827), Kasiprasad Ghose's *The Shair or Minstrel and Other Poems* (1830), Michael Madhusudan Dutt's *The Captive Ladie* (1849) and Manmohan Ghose's *Love Songs and Elegies* (1898) are today only of historical interest.

Toru Dutt (1856–77) has an undisputed claim to be regarded as the first Indian poet in English. She put the emphasis back on India, although her verse often glows with English romanticism of the mid-

nineteenth century. In 'Our Casuarina Tree', the tree in the family
home at Baugmaree where she lived till the age of twelve is invested
with the glamour of an Indian childhood, laced with thin reminiscences of English and French literature:

> But not because of its magnificence
>   Dear is the Casuarina to my soul:
>   Beneath it we have played; though years may roll,
> O sweet companions, loved with love intense,
>   For your sakes shall the tree be ever dear!
> Blent with your images, it shall arise
> In memory, till the hot tears blind mine eyes!

Residence in England only increased her awareness of the India she
was familiar with. The success of the poem lies in the concretization
of something as amorphous as nostalgia which is a common enough
experience of all exiles.

Of those who wrote in the first half of the twentieth century, again,
only a few are remembered: Aurobindo Ghose, Sarojini Naidu,
Joseph Furtado and Harindranath Chattopadhyaya. Their output
was prolific—Aurobindo Ghose's *Savitri* (1951) alone comprises 24,000
lines—and it was throughout uneven in quality. Today, one seriously
questions their outsize reputations.

In *Savitri*, Ghose attempted to 'catch something of the Upanishadic
movement so far as that is possible in English'. But *Savitri* fails as a
poem because Ghose's talent and resourcefulness in the use of English
were limited. Far from plugging the holes in the umbrella, he sprang
a leak which, even twenty-five years after his death, has been only
partially stopped.

> Man, sole awake in an unconscious world,
> Aspires in vain to change the cosmic dream.
> Arrived from some half-luminous Beyond
> He is a stranger in the mindless vasts;
> A traveller in his oft-shifting home
> Amid the tread of many infinitudes,
> He has pitched a tent of life in desert Space.

Sarojini Naidu (1879–1949) had on the other hand perhaps the
finest ear among Indian poets for the sound of English. In 'Palanquin-
bearers', for example, the springy and elastic steps are echoed by
the anapaestic metre:

> Lightly, O lightly, we bear her along,
> She sways like a flower in the wind of our song;

She skims like a bird on the foam of a stream,
She floats like a laugh on the lips of a dream.
Gaily, O gaily, we glide and we sing,
We bear her along like a pearl on a string.

Prosodically, her verse is excellent; as poetry, it disappoints. In spite of her having pumped enough feeling into them, the poems invariably have trouble getting started. However, posterity appears to have taken more kindly to her than to Toru Dutt.

Toru Dutt's poems mean little to us because our idea of poetry has changed since her day. This raises a crucial question: can we know outside or beyond our own era's ideas about language? There is a conflict between language as a simple communication and man's desire for ever greater expressiveness—a conflict between informing on the one hand and, on the other, trying through language to put something new or personal in the world, to use words in unaccustomed ways.

3

In examining the phenomenon of Indian verse in English, one comes up, first of all, against the paradox that it did not seriously begin to exist till after the withdrawal of the British from India. An important characteristic of Indian verse in English in the mid-twentieth century has been its emergence from the mainstream of English literature and its appearance as part of Indian literature. It has been said that it is Indian in sensibility and content, and English in language. It is rooted in and stems from the Indian environment, and reflects its mores, often ironically.

However, for an Indian writing in English, there are at least two problems. And, sooner or later, he has to come to terms with them. The first is the quality of experience he would like to express in English. The Indian who uses the English language feels, to some extent, alienated. His development as a poet is sporadic. And it is partly because of this that there is, today, no perspective at all in which to evaluate this phenomenon. The second is the quality of the idiom he uses. There has always been a time-lag between the living, creative idiom of English-speaking peoples and the English used in India. And this time-lag is not likely to diminish, although it has today considerably narrowed down. It is true that the historical situation is to blame. Besides, there is no special Indian-English idiom, either. English in India rarely approaches the liveliness and idiosyncracy of usage one finds in African or West Indian writing, perhaps because of the long traditions of literatures in the Indian languages, and also because of the relative sophistication of those who write in English. It is not surprising, therefore, that writers in English are conscious of their Indianness because, at the bottom of it all, one suspects a crisis of identity. This explains why Michael Madhusudan Dutt (1824–73), after publishing his first book of verse, *The Captive Ladie* (1849), in English turned to Bengali in which he wrote *Meghanadbadh Kavya* (1861). He is the paradigm of the Indian poet writing in English. He exemplifies the uneasy tensions that arose in using a language he wasn't born into, and which he abandoned at the age of thirty-five to write in his own language. Fernando Pessoa (1888–1935) is, perhaps, the supreme example in poetry of the phenomenon of bilingualism. After writing exclusively in English till the age of twenty-one, he started writing in Portuguese to become one of the greatest poets in that language since Camoens.

The impact of the West on Indian languages has been extraordinarily productive. In the nineteenth century, educated Indians responded to Western thought and literature. They critically examined the foundations of their own society and culture, and formulated proposals for social and religious reform. Their efforts found expression in both English and the Indian languages, especially Bengali. From 1773 to 1911, Calcutta was the capital of British India. This led to the Bengali intelligentsia being exposed the longest to the West. The repercussions of this exposure appeared unmistakably in Bengali literature.

Of the poets included here, eight are truly bilingual. Besides English, they also write in an Indian language or translate from it into English. Kolatkar, for instance, writes cryptic, often aphoristic, poems in both English and Marathi with equal competence. His poems in Marathi are in the tradition of the bhakti poets, especially Tukaram whom he has translated into English. 'The Seventeen Lions Congealed'[1] has a pronounced surrealistic flavour, something new in Marathi verse.

> The seventeen lions congealed
> In a carpet are delivered
> In the void of the woman's body
> Hanging by a rope
>
> The goat of glass in the corner
> Takes a metaphysical leap
> Transcends the barrier
> Of the hanged woman's body
>
> The empty vase flashes
> Like the flashgun of a camera

[1] In *An Anthology of Marathi Poetry 1945–65*, ed. Dilip Chitre (Bombay, 1967).

And like the heavenly negatives
Of the snap of a suicide

Issues flowers of blinding light
Which burn the spectator's eyes

It is interesting to note that Kolatkar does not use English and
Marathi for different purposes. This becomes obvious when one
compares his poems written in English with those translated into
English from Marathi. A truly bilingual poet, Kolatkar is in a class
by himself. His is the fortunate, middle position. Those who favour
writing only in English or in an Indian language after having written
in English for a considerable time represent the two other positions.
Most of the poets in this book are somewhere between these two
positions.

Thus, the poets are intensely aware of the unenviable situation in
which they function, and the situation itself has been exploited by
not a few of them. Their work exemplifies both the problems and
the specific achievement of Indian verse in English.

4

Any evaluation of Indian verse in English is usually bedevilled by
the question of national identity. Many of the poets in this selection
will be found to be preoccupied with it. Ezekiel states his position
honestly and without rhetoric:

India is simply my environment. A man can do something for and
in his environment by being fully what he is, by not withdrawing
from it. I have not withdrawn from India.[1]

In the poem, 'Entertainment', we see a measure of his involvement.
Incidentally, he also encapsulates the 'boring minutiae of suburban
and urban existence'.

Only the monkeys are sad,
and suddenly
the baby begins to cry.
Anticipating time for payment,
the crowd dissolves,
some, in shame, part
with the smallest coin they have.
The show moves on.

The movement of the poem is throughout linear, but towards the end

[1] Nissim Ezekiel, 'Naipaul's India and Mine', *New Writing in India*, ed. Adil
Jussawalla (Harmondsworth, 1974), 88.

it curves abruptly, almost turning a somersault. Something as un-
eventful as a monkey show has provoked Ezekiel to an ironic social
comment.

In fact, it is through irony that the poet comes to grips with the
essential ambivalence of the Indian situation. Shanmuga Subbiah
(b. 1924), in his Tamil poem 'Dog Show',[1] a poem similar to Ezekiel's,
achieves the same effect:

> I too saw
> the dog show.
> It was amusing.
>
> But coming out
> I walked into a crowd
> of pariah dogs.

Like Ezekiel, Daruwalla is intensely aware of his environment. He
tries to restore order in the chaos he finds around him with the heal-
ing touch of irony.

> The river calls: clay-lamp and libation
> offered to the eclipse to release the sun.
> Ghats aflame with the dead.
> Sorry, we can't lay on these days
> a suttee-display in the flesh for you.
>
> ('To Writers Abroad')

Mahapatra observes similar incongruities in the Indian landscape:

> Endless crow noises.
> A skull on the holy sands
> tilts its empty country towards hunger.
>
> ('Dawn at Puri')

What he writes of Orissa is true of the rest of the country:

A kind of struggle floats in the air and laps the hearts of men: the
struggle just to live, against drought and floods, storm and fever.
Nothing more.[2]

This is in striking contrast to the poets of the nineteenth century

---

[1] In *Kurukshetram*, ed. Nakulan (Madras, 1968). Reprinted by permission of
the author and the publishers.
[2] Jayanta Mahapatra, 'An Orissa Journal: July to November 1972', *Queen's
Quarterly*, Vol. 80, No. 1 (Spring, 1973), 65.

who were more interested in traditional India, as Toru Dutt's *Ancient Ballads and Legends of Hindustan* (1882) testifies.

5

One of the basic problems for the poets has been to find an adequate and, above all, a personal language. A few have been successful. But, by and large, they have not been able to extend the resources of the English language or even to Indianize it. However, there are two outstanding exceptions in fiction: Raja Rao's *Kanthapura* (1938) and G. V. Desani's *All About H. Hatterr* (1948). Rao's and Desani's idiolects are the most impressive and enduring achievements of the two novels. In Desani's case, it comprises cliché, slang and ejaculatory phrases which are his own invention.

Once, in India, I developed a hell of a passion for maps—a literal mapomania!
'Mr H. Hatterr,' said the feller, reproaching, 'my heart bleeds at the way you spend your hard-earned lucre on maps. You are neglecting your personal appearance. Your beard is grown. And he has said, Alas, poor chin! Many a wart is richer! Your pants are patched. You spend your money on maps, amounts which could be better employed in purchasing essential oils, and vitamins and minerals, for your daily intake. Excuse me, but you need nourishment. I am deeply grieved.'

No one has, to the same extent, taken comparable risks in verse. And the first poet to try—and this was in the 1920s—was Joseph Furtado (1872–1947). He wrote some poems in pidgin or bazaar English, like 'The Fortune-teller' and 'Lakshmi'. But Furtado himself did not use pidgin English extensively, except in a few humorous poems. He was interested in it as a source of humour. He seemed to have been unaware of the possibility of its developing into a creole. A pidgin, in any case, arises under the pressure of practical circumstances in a bilingual situation.

Goan Fiddler: O meri rani, hamko do toda pani.
Lakshmi: I speaking English, saib.
Goan Fiddler: Very well, my English-speaking daughter, give me then a little water.
Lakshmi: Why little? Drink plenty much. All peoples liking water of this well.
Goan Fiddler: Many thanks. Never thought to find in this out-of-the-way village a Hindu girl speaking English. And nice English too you speak, my daughter.
Lakshmi: I going to English School in Poona. 'Smart thing that goldsmith's daughter', teacher always saying. I no girl, saib, I marry.

Goan Fiddler: I know it, and have a child too—quite a beauty like its mother. You must let me see it.
Lakshmi: No, no, I have not got child, saib. You make me quite shame. Where you going, saib?

('Lakshmi')

After Furtado, Ezekiel is the only poet to have seriously considered the use of pidgin English, notably in poems like 'A Very Indian Poem in Indian English', 'Goodbye Party for Miss Pushpa T. S.' and 'The Professor'. These poems imitate the idiolectal features of English used by Gujarati speakers. Some of these features are also present in other Indian languages: the use of the present progressive tense for the simple present tense, un-English collocation of lexical items, and literal translation of phrases and idioms. All these features show up in these lines from 'The Professor':

If you are coming again this side by chance,
Visit please my humble residence also.
I am living just on opposite house's backside.

This is the unmistakable jargon of the *métèque* who uses English in defiance of the rules of idiom and grammar. In the absence of a linguistically respectable variety of Indian English, the jargon never rises above caricature. In fact, the jargon is heard all over the Sub-continent. The Sinhalese poet, Tilak Gunawardena (b. 1940), uses it for its humour in 'Ballad for Paradise Island', an exposé of 'Ceylon hospitality':

What I say is, everywhere the money's getting tight:
Every night reminding Joe to off the electric light.
When these fellers coming here and
Giving us a helping hand,
Well, why our people treating them as if they going to bite?

But our use of pidgin English, as exemplified by Furtado and Ezekiel, has none of the colloquial reverberations one encounters in African usage as, for instance, in 'One Wife for One Man' by Frank Aig-Imoukhuede (b. 1935), one of the first Nigerian poets to attempt writing in pidgin English.

My fader before my fader get him wife borku.[1]
E no' get equality palaver; he live well
For he be oga[2] for im own house.
But dat time done pass before white man come
Wit 'im
One wife for one man.

[1] borku = plenty. [2] oga = master or lord.

Pidgin English in India is not part of the spoken idiom as it is in
Africa. For this reason Furtado's and Ezekiel's use of it stops at
parody.

Without resorting to pidgin, Ramanujan on the other hand has
been able to forge an oblique, elliptical style all his own.

> No, not only prophets
> walk on water. This bug sits
> on a landslide of lights
> and drowns eye-
> deep
> into its tiny strip
> of sky.

('The Striders')

Furthermore, English being a foreign language, the words are not
burdened with irrelevant associations for the poet. They are invariably ordinary and inconspicuous; rarely, if ever, reverberant. And
herein lies their strength. There is something clinical about Ramanujan's use of the language. It has a cold, glass-like quality. It is an
attempt to turn language into an artifact.

All the poets, however, use the tones and rhythms of familiar,
everyday speech, and employ cliché and slang in incongruous con-
texts to achieve unexpected effects.

6

In Ramanujan, Kolatkar, Mehrotra and Kumar, the image is not
only the spring-board of poetic composition, but the kernel as well.
Underneath the poems one can decipher the pattern in which they
seem to think—the pattern of images. Thus, their basic means of
expression is subliminal, and it lies below the threshold of language.
The images are primarily visual. Words tend to collocate together
into an image which then triggers off the poem. The entire poem is,
in fact, one image or a complex of more than one image. It is in this
context that the use of the image is seminal. In our time poetry is
becoming increasingly concise. It is moving towards metaphor and
away from comparison: poetry, essentially as metaphor.

> The entire island:
> an alligator
> sleeping in a mask of stone.
> A grin of land
>
> even on good days; on bad,
> the ocean foams in that mouth.

(Ramanujan: 'No Man Is an Island')

and swears
at the seagull
who invents
on the spur of the air
what is clearly the whitest inflection
known . . .

(Kolatkar: 'the boatride')

Be careful, one river is still wet
and slippery; its waters continue to
run like footprints . . .
        I have a map left, drawn
by migrating birds.

(Mehrotra: 'The Sale')

Patiently they sit
like empty pitchers
on the mouth of the village well
pleating hope in each braid
of their mississippi-long hair . . .

(Kumar: 'Indian Women')

7

Apart from Ezekiel, the poets have little or no use for traditional
English prosody, though five of them have had formal training in
English literature. This isn't as surprising as it may appear. Prosody
is essentially aural, and requires a keen ear. And not all the poets
possess it. The emphasis is, therefore, almost entirely on the visual
as opposed to the aural element in verse. Only Ezekiel handles both
metre and rhyme as well as free verse with skill.

There is a place to which I often go,
Not by planning to, but by a flow
Away from all existence, to a cold
Lucidity, whose will is uncontrolled.
Here, the mills of God are never slow.

('Philosophy')

The ease with which he is able to modulate one of the commonest of
English measures, the couplet, is commendable. The couplets here
are open, with the thought overflowing from the second rhyme into
the following line. The rhythm swerves in an arc undisturbed, till
the last line—echoing the rhyme in the beginning—brings it to a
close.

In spite of the absence of special prosodic features, for example, metre and rhyme, one feature appears rather prominently: most of the poets favour a short as opposed to a long line as the unit of composition. The line is easily spoken in one effort of the breath. Often, the line breaks abruptly, only to seek a balance outside itself.

> They sit like animals.
> I mean no offence. I have seen
> Animals resting in their stall,
> The oil flame reflected in their eyes,
> Large beads that though protruding
> Actually rest
> Behind the regular grind
> Of the jaws.
>
> (Patel: 'Servants')

> When I got married
> my husband said,
> you may have freedom,
> as much as you want.
> My soul balked at this diet of ash.
> Freedom became my dancing shoe,
> how well I danced,
> and danced without rest,
> until the shoes turned grimy on my feet ...
>
> (Kamala Das: 'Composition')

8

The fifty odd poems brought together here for the first time indicate the directions Indian verse in English has taken in the past twenty-five years. It is, perhaps, too early to forecast the influence they are likely to have on its future development. In the context of Indian verse as a whole, the contribution of poets writing in English is only marginal, and is likely to remain so. But it can, today, be unreservedly said that it is a significant contribution in that it is a legitimate expression of universal, human experience.

Every poet, sooner or later, suffers from aphasia or loss of poetic speech. Rather than let it happen unexpectedly, his poetry should from the beginning aspire to the condition of silence. A poem ought to, in effect, try to arrest the flow of language, to anaesthetize it, to petrify it, to fossilize it. Ultimately, it is the reader who breathes life into the poem, awakening it from its enforced sleep in the language.

Keki N. Daruwalla

Keki Nasserwanji Daruwalla was born in Lahore in 1937, and was educated at Government College, Ludhiana. He currently lives in New Delhi. His works include *Under Orion* (1970) and *Apparition in April* (1971), for which he was given the Uttar Pradesh State Award in 1972 and *Crossing of Rivers*, 1976. He has contributed to *Opinion*, *Poetry Australia* (Sydney), *Transatlantic Review* (London) and *TriQuarterly* (Evanston, Illinois).

Daruwalla has been praised for his bitter, satiric tone, which is rather exceptional in Indian verse in English. Instances may be cited from *Under Orion:* 'Dialogues with a Third Voice', 'Collage 1' and 'Death by Burial'.

> My conscience is a road—
> a childhood has been trampled here
> concretized and stamped over
> with the feet of passing years.
> We erode each other, the road and I
> neither giving way,
> I scrape the road's back as I walk,
> my heel is horned
> calloused and worn away.

('Dialogues with a Third Voice')

The landscape of northern India—hills, plains and rivers—is evoked in many poems, notably in 'The Ghaghra in Spate', where the 'terror of the villagers at night as they fought the river' is recorded with compassion and understanding. Daruwalla writes, 'I am not an urban writer and my poems are rooted in the rural landscape. My poetry is earthy, and I like to consciously keep it that way, shunning sophistication which, while adding gloss, takes away from the power of verse.' There is an obviously Indian element in Daruwalla's verse, especially in his use of the landscape. When it isn't ornamental, the landscape comes alive as a presence on its own. The language then is pared to the bone. Images are concrete and exact.

'Writing a poem', says Daruwalla, 'is like a clot going out of the blood.' This is true of a poem like 'Death of a Bird' which has an intensity, a thrust that makes it a significant experience.

from THE EPILEPTIC

1

Suddenly the two children
flew from her side
    like severed wings.

Thank God, the burden in her belly
stayed where it was.

The rickshaw-puller was a study in guilt.
It was too much for him:
the convulsionary and her frightened kids
floundering about in a swarm of limbs.

A focus in the brain
    or some such flap,
the look had gone from the mother's eyes
the way her children
    had flown from her lap.

The husband dug through the mound
that was her face; forced the mouth wide
plucked out the receding tongue
    warped into a clotted wound
    and put a gag between her teeth.

The traffic ground
to an inquisitive halt. A crowd senses
a mishap before it sees one.
They fanned her, rubbed her feet, and looked around
for other ways to summon back her senses.
A pedestrian whispered,
'Her seizures are cyclic;
they visit her in her menses.'

She was not hysteric, she didn't rave,
her face was flushed, abstract, the marionette-
head jerked from side to side, a slave

to cross-pulls. A thin edge of froth
simmered round her lips
like foam-dregs left by a receding wave.

The hospital doctors frowned with thought:
light words like *petit mal* were tied
to the heavies, psychomotor epilepsy.
A physician pointed out with pride
the 'spike-and-wave' electrical activity,
prescribed belladonna and paraldehyde.

Just when he said, 'She isn't shaping
too well', she recovered, bleached
        by the sun of her agony.
As a limp awareness slouched along her face
I found it was the husband who was shaking.

THE GHAGHRA IN SPATE

And every year
the Ghaghra changes course
turning over and over in her sleep.

In the afternoon she is a grey smudge
exploring a grey canvas.
When dusk reaches her
through an overhang of cloud
she is overstewed coffee.
At night under a red moon in menses
she is a red weal
across the spine of the land.

Driving at dusk you wouldn't know
there's a flood 'on':
the landscape is so superbly equipoised—
rice-shoots pricking through

a stretch of water and light
spiked shadows
   inverted trees
      kingfishers, gulls.
  As twilight thins
 the road is a black stretch
running between the stars.

And suddenly at night
the north comes to the village
riding on river-back.
Twenty minutes of a nightmare spin
and fear turns phantasmal
as half a street goes
churning in the river-belly.
If only voices could light lamps!
If only limbs could turn to rafted bamboo!

And through the village
the Ghaghra steers her course:
thatch and dung-cakes turn to river-scum,
a buffalo floats over to the rooftop
where the men are stranded.
Three days of hunger, and her udders
turn red-rimmed and swollen
    with milk-extortion.

Children have spirit enough in them
to cheer the rescue boats;
the men are still-life subjects
   oozing wet looks.
They don't rave or curse
for they know the river's slang, her argot.
No one sends prayers to a wasted sky
for prayers are parabolic:
they will come down with a plop anyway.
Instead there's a slush-stampede
outside the booth
where they are doling out salt and grain.

Ten miles to her flank
peasants go fishing in rice-fields
and women in chauffeur-driven cars
go looking for driftwood.

But it's when she recedes
that the Ghaghra turns bitchy
sucking with animal-heat,
cross-eddies diving like frogmen
and sawing away the waterfront
in a paranoid frenzy.
She flees from the scene of her own havoc
arms akimbo, thrashing with pain.
Behind her the land sinks,
houses sag on to their knees
in a farewell obeisance.
And miles to the flank, the paddy fields
will hoard their fish
till the mud enters into
a conspiracy with the sun
and strangles them.

from RUMINATIONS

1

I can smell violence in the air
like the lash of coming rain—
mass hatreds drifting grey across the moon.

It hovers brooding, poised like a cobra
as I go prodding rat-holes
and sounding caverns
looking for a fang that darts,
a hood that sways
and eyes that squirt a reptile hate.

I watch my wounds but they don't turn green.
Cross-bones I look for you!
Death I am looking
for that bald bone-head of yours!

But it's in flesh and flesh-tissue
    that my destiny lies
and slowly corruption takes a hold.
Over from the mortuary
    comes the corpse-drift.
(Death is so soft, put it ten days in a well
    and it turns pulpy.)
Rosewater, incense-sticks, flowers—
the relatives have done their bit.
The drift as it comes to us now
is aroma/stench/nausea
jostling each other!
In the morgue-verandah another queues up,
her nose sliced off, her lung punctured.
(It is a three-word story:
infidelity—irate husband.)

Man is so pliant, adaptable. Bury him
and he is steadfast as the earth.
Burn him and he will ride the flames.
Throw him to the birds and he will
surrender flesh like an ascetic.

Rain comes clamouring down,
a blind sheet of water.
Once the blur lifts
colours deepen, the hedge smiles,
the leaf loses its coat of dust,
the scum spills over from the pool.
I look around for a cleansed feeling,
the kind you experience
walking in a temple
after a river-bath.
I cannot find it.
I have misplaced it somewhere
in the caverns of my past.

KEKI N. DARUWALLA

FIRE-HYMN

The burning ghat erupted phosphorescence:
and wandering ghost-lights frightened passers-by
as moonlight scuttled among the bones.
Once strolling at dawn past river-bank and ghat
we saw embers losing their cruel redness
to the grey ash that swallows all. Half-cooked limbs
bore witness to the fire's debauchery.
My father said, 'You see those half-burnt fingers
and bone-stubs? The fire at times forgets its dead!'
A Zoroastrian I, my child-fingers clenched
into a little knot of pain,
I swore to save fire
from the sin of forgetfulness.

It never forgot, and twenty years since
as I consigned my first-born to the flames—
the nearest Tower of Silence[1] was a thousand miles—
the fire-hymn said to me, 'You stand forgiven.'
Broken, yet rebellious, I swore this time
to save it from the sin of forgiving.

ROUTINE

The putties were left behind by the Raj
a strip of fire round the legs in June.
Within the burning crash-helmet
the brain is a fire-pulp. The asphalt
gives way beneath our boots and sticks.
The edges of the crowd give way;
a ring of abuse re-forms behind us.
We hardly hear them for we are used to it.
Their gamut ranges from 'mother-' to 'sister-seducer'.

[1] Structure on which the Parsis expose their dead.

Karam Singh marching in the same rank as I
curses under his breath,
'I have children older than them,
these kids whose pubes have hardly sprouted!'

We march to the street-crossing where young blood
fulfils itself by burning tramcars.
Beneath our khaki we are a roasted brown
but unconvinced, they wish to burn our khaki skins.
We are a platoon against a thousand.
It's all well rehearsed; a few words of warning—
a chill formality lost in fiery slogans!
'Load!' I put a piece of death up the spout.
It is well rehearsed: I alone point
my barrel into them as I squeeze the trigger.
The rest aim into the sun!

They have gone. The Salvage Squad comes
and takes the body to the autopsy room
and tows the tramcar away.
Tension oozes out as armpits run with sweat.
Depressed and weary we march back to the Lines.
A leader says over the evening wireless,
'We are marching forward.'

DEATH OF A BIRD

Under an overhang of crags
fierce bird-love:
the monals mated, clawed and screamed;
the female brown and nondescript
the male was king, a fire-dream!
My barrel spoke one word of lead:
the bird came down, the king was dead,

or almost dying:
his eyes were glazed, the breast still throbbed.

We tucked him pulsing as he was in our rucksack.
The female rose, in terror crying!
With bird-blood on our hands we walked,
and as the skies broke into rags
of mist, why did our footsteps drag?

The cumulus piled on the crags.
We smote the pony on its shanks
to hurry him; around a bend
he swivelled and went down the flank
of rock a thousand feet below
to where the roaring river flowed.

His scream
climbed up the gorge, a nightmare fang
which ploughed my blistered dreams and sowed
begging children.
Depressed a bit we took the road;
walking like ciphers disinterred
from some forgotten code.

Dusk caught up with us, and bears;
my terror-gun spat at the shades
but missed each time.
When jackals howled, sniffing my ribs
trembling she asked if they were wolves?
I simply held her hand in mine
and walked on further to a cave
hemmed in by pine we would have missed
but for a growling *bhotia* dog
the resin-tappers left behind
to guard their cans and beaded ichor
pimpling like a spray of cysts.
Just yards off an escarpment wrote
hieroglyphs on a scroll of mist.

And as she crumpled with a chill
I lit a fire of turf and peat
and rubbed her clotted sides and feet
and found her waking in my hands

(this shadow-pair of quickening hands)
like embers in a shadow-net.
In the wet lanes of her body
we, apprehensive, met.

And as we rose to the final kill—
two electric saws meeting on a hill
in the narrowing bones of a fractured tree—
each of us thought the other was free
of the pony's scream and the monal's wings
and the prowling bears in the firelight-rim.

Her head on my heartbeat, hair locked in my fingers
she purred into sleep; the night seemed to flower
late with our dreams
for the moon came out just for an hour or two
and the monal-wings came feathering down
in a passion of dusky gold and blue.
And the wolves, with the mist, went over the cliff—
but for the wind we both would have dreamt
the very same dream of quiescence and love;
but the wind was a thorn in the flesh of the night
and moaned aloud like a witch in the flue.

I broke my gun in two across the back
of an ash-grey dawn. A brown bird left the crags
flying strongly, and as its shadow crossed us
it shrieked with fear and turned to stone
dropping at our feet.
'It's the queen-monal! We are accursed!' she said.
'Just watch its eyes!' For though the bird was near dead
its eyes flared terror like bits of dripping meat!

Kamala Das

Kamala Das was born at Punnayurkulam in southern Malabar in 1934, and was educated mainly at home. She lives in Bombay. A bilingual writer, her works in English and Malayalam include *Summer in Calcutta* (1965), *The Descendants* (1967), *The Old Playhouse and Other Poems* (1973) and *My Story* (1975), an autobiography. A few of her stories, originally written in Malayalam, are published in *Modern Indian Short Stories: An Anthology* (1974). She was given the Poetry Award of *The Asian PEN Anthology* in 1964 and the Kerala Sahitya Akademi Award in 1969 for *Cold*, a collection of short stories in Malayalam. Her poems have appeared in *Opinion, New Writing in India* (Penguin Books, 1974) and *Young Commonwealth Poets '65* (Heinemann, 1965).

With a frankness and openness unusual in the Indian context, Kamala Das expresses her need for love. What is overpowering about her poems is their sense of urgency. They literally boil over, for instance, 'The Old Playhouse', 'The Looking-glass' and 'The Freaks'. In 'Substitute' she tells us rather cynically what her experience of love turned out to be:

> After that love became a swivel-door,
> When one went out, another came in.

The despair is infectious. Few of her poems have, in fact, escaped it. In 'An Introduction' it provides a focus for an exercise in autobiography.

On the other hand, her reminiscences of childhood at Nalapat House, her family home, are tinged with nostalgia, as in 'A Hot Noon in Malabar' and 'My Grandmother's House'. She writes, 'From every city I have lived I have remembered the noons in Malabar with an ache growing inside me, a homesickness.' Kamala Das impresses by being very much herself in her poems. The tone is distinctively feminine.

THE FREAKS

He talks, turning a sun-stained
Cheek to me, his mouth, a dark
Cavern, where stalactites of
Uneven teeth gleam, his right
Hand on my knee, while our minds
Are willed to race towards love;
But, they only wander, tripping
Idly over puddles of
Desire. . . . Can't this man with
Nimble finger-tips unleash
Nothing more alive than the
Skin's lazy hungers? Who can
Help us who have lived so long
And have failed in love? The heart,
An empty cistern, waiting
Through long hours, fills itself
With coiling snakes of silence. . . .
I am a freak. It's only
To save my face, I flaunt, at
Times, a grand, flamboyant lust.

MY GRANDMOTHER'S HOUSE

There is a house now far away where once
I received love. . . . That woman died,
The house withdrew into silence, snakes moved
Among books I was then too young
To read, and my blood turned cold like the moon.
How often I think of going
There, to peer through blind eyes of windows or
Just listen to the frozen air,
Or in wild despair, pick an armful of
Darkness to bring it here to lie

Behind my bedroom door like a brooding
Dog . . . you cannot believe, darling,
Can you, that I lived in such a house and
Was proud, and loved . . . I who have lost
My way and beg now at strangers' doors to
Receive love, at least in small change?

A HOT NOON IN MALABAR

This is a noon for beggars with whining
Voices, a noon for men who come from hills
With parrots in a cage and fortune-cards,
All stained with time, for brown *Kurava*[1] girls
With old eyes, who read palms in light singsong
Voices, for bangle-sellers who spread
On the cool black floor those red and green and blue
Bangles, all covered with the dust of roads,
For all of them, whose feet, devouring rough
Miles, grow cracks on the heels, so that when they
Clambered up our porch, the noise was grating,
Strange. . . . This is a noon for strangers who part
The window-drapes and peer in, their hot eyes
Brimming with the sun, not seeing a thing in
Shadowy rooms and turn away and look
So yearningly at the brick-ledged well. This
Is a noon for strangers with mistrust in
Their eyes, dark, silent ones who rarely speak
At all, so that when they speak, their voices
Run wild, like jungle-voices. Yes, this is
A noon for wild men, wild thoughts, wild love. To
Be here, far away, is torture. Wild feet
Stirring up the dust, this hot noon, at my
Home in Malabar, and I so far away. . . .

---

[1] Caste of fowlers, basket-makers and fortune-tellers.

THE SUNSHINE CAT

They did this to her, the men who knew her, the man
She loved, who loved her not enough, being selfish
And a coward, the husband who neither loved nor
Used her, but was a ruthless watcher, and the band
Of cynics she turned to, clinging to their chests where
New hair sprouted like great-winged moths, burrowing her
Face into their smells and their young lusts to forget,
To forget, oh, to forget . . . and, they said, each of
Them, I do not love, I cannot love, it is not
In my nature to love, but I can be kind to you. . . .
They let her slide from pegs of sanity into
A bed made soft with tears and she lay there weeping,
For sleep had lost its use; I shall build walls with tears,
She said, walls to shut me in. . . . Her husband shut her
In every morning; locked her in a room of books
With a streak of sunshine lying near the door, like
A yellow cat, to keep her company, but soon,
Winter came and one day while locking her in, he
Noticed that the cat of sunshine was only a
Line, a hair-thin line, and in the evening when
He returned to take her out, she was a cold and
Half-dead woman, now of no use at all to men.

THE INVITATION

I have a man's fist in my head today
Clenching, unclenching. . . .
I have got all the Sunday evening pains.

The sea is garrulous today. Come in,
Come in. What do you lose by dying, and
Besides, your losses are my gains.

Oh sea, let me shrink or grow, slosh up,
Slide down, go your way.

I will go mine. He came to me between
Long conferences, a fish coming up
For air, and was warm in my arms
And inarticulate. . . . You are diseased
With remembering,
The man is gone for good. It would indeed
Be silly to wait for his returning.
Come in, come in. Oh sea, just leave
Me alone. As long
As I remember, I want no other.
On the bed with him, the boundaries of
Paradise had shrunk to a mere
Six by two and afterwards, when we walked
Out together, they
Widened to hold the unknowing city. . . .
End in me, cries the sea. Think of yourself
Lying on a funeral pyre
With a burning head. Just think. Bathe cool,
Stretch your limbs on cool
Secret sands, pillow your head on anemones.
All through that summer's afternoons we lay
On beds, our limbs inert, cells expanding
Into throbbing suns. The heat had
Blotted our thoughts. . . . Please end this whiplash
Of memories, cries
The sea. For long I've waited for the right one
To come, the bright one, the right one to live
In the blue. No. I am still young
And I need that man for construction and
Destruction. Leave me. . . .
The sea shall bear some prying and certain
Violations, but I tell you, the sea
Shall take no more, the sea shall take
No more. . . . The tides beat against the walls, they
Beat in childish rage. . . .
Darling, forgive, how long can one resist?

THE LOOKING-GLASS

Getting a man to love you is easy
Only be honest about your wants as
Woman. Stand nude before the glass with him
So that he sees himself the stronger one
And believes it so, and you so much more
Softer, younger, lovelier. . . . Admit your
Admiration. Notice the perfection
Of his limbs, his eyes reddening under
The shower, the shy walk across the bathroom floor,
Dropping towels, and the jerky way he
Urinates. All the fond details that make
Him male and your only man. Gift him all,
Gift him what makes you woman, the scent of
Long hair, the musk of sweat between the breasts,
The warm shock of menstrual blood, and all your
Endless female hungers. Oh yes, getting
A man to love is easy, but living
Without him afterwards may have to be
Faced. A living without life when you move
Around, meeting strangers, with your eyes that
Gave up their search, with ears that hear only
His last voice calling out your name and your
Body which once under his touch had gleamed
Like burnished brass, now drab and destitute.

Nissim Ezekiel

Nissim Ezekiel was born in Bombay in 1924, and was educated at Antonio D'Souza High School and Wilson College, Bombay and Birkbeck College, London. He lives in Bombay, where he is Reader in American Literature at the University. In 1964, he was a Visiting Professor at Leeds University; in 1974, an invitee of the U.S. government under its International Visitors Program; and in 1975, a Cultural Award Visitor to Australia. For some time he was Director of Theatre Unit, Bombay. His works include *A Time to Change* (1952), *Sixty Poems* (1953), *The Third* (1959), *The Unfinished Man* (1960), *The Exact Name* (1965), *Three Plays* (1969) and *Snakeskin and Other Poems* (1974), translations from the Marathi of Indira Sant and *Hymns in Darkness* (1976). He has had poems published in *Encounter*, *The Illustrated Weekly of India*, *London Magazine* and *The Spectator*.

Ezekiel's poetry is both the instrument and the outcome of his attempt as a man to come to terms with himself. One finds in the poems the imprint of a keen, analytical mind trying to explore and communicate on a personal level feelings of loss and deprivation. 'Scores of my poems', he says, 'are obviously written for personal, therapeutic purposes.' One such instance is 'Enterprise'. A situation is examined with ironic detachment in the hope that it would offer release. This seldom happens, but he persists in the exercise. Again, he says of himself, 'I am not a Hindu, and my background makes me a natural outsider: circumstances and decisions relate me to India.' In 'Background, Casually', he states his case unambiguously.

'Night of the Scorpion' evokes superstitious practices we haven't still outgrown. It enacts an impressive ritual in which the mother's reaction, towards the end, to her own suffering ironically cancels out earlier responses, both primitive and sophisticated. The inter-relationship between the domestic tragedy and the surrounding community is unobtrusively established. The poem also demonstrates the effective use of parallelism.

In 'Poet, Lover, Birdwatcher', the search for love and the word is presented in the person of a birdwatcher. The image is appropriate in the context, where it helps to control a 'potentially explosive situation'. Both love and words visit the poet without his knowledge. There is no pursuit, only waiting. In fact, the waiting itself becomes a form of pursuit, a strategy. It is only then that the revelation occurs. The analogies, separately explored, now come together, and the metaphor used to suggest this fusion is light. In 'Poetry as Knowledge', Ezekiel tells us, 'What the poet knows makes the poem what it is, if the poet's knowledge is alive and his art fully extended while he writes the poem.' 'Poet, Lover, Birdwatcher' epitomizes Ezekiel's search for a poetics which would help him redeem himself in his eyes and in the eyes of God. For an explication of 'Poet, Lover, Birdwatcher', see Meena Belliappa in *The Miscellany* (1971: No. 46).

NISSIM EZEKIEL

ENTERPRISE

It started as a pilgrimage,
Exalting minds and making all
The burdens light. The second stage
Explored but did not test the call.
The sun beat down to match our rage.

We stood it very well, I thought,
Observed and put down copious notes
On things the peasants sold and bought,
The way of serpents and of goats,
Three cities where a sage had taught.

But when the differences arose
On how to cross a desert patch,
We lost a friend whose stylish prose
Was quite the best of all our batch.
A shadow falls on us—and grows.

Another phase was reached when we
Were twice attacked, and lost our way.
A section claimed its liberty
To leave the group. I tried to pray.
Our leader said he smelt the sea.

We noticed nothing as we went,
A straggling crowd of little hope,
Ignoring what the thunder meant,
Deprived of common needs like soap.
Some were broken, some merely bent.

When, finally, we reached the place,
We hardly knew why we were there.
The trip had darkened every face,
Our deeds were neither great nor rare.
Home is where we have to gather grace.

PHILOSOPHY

There is a place to which I often go,
Not by planning to, but by a flow
Away from all existence, to a cold
Lucidity, whose will is uncontrolled.
Here, the mills of God are never slow.

The landscape in its geologic prime
Dissolves to show its quintessential slime.
A million stars are blotted out. I think
Of each historic passion as a blink
That happened to the sad eye of Time.

But residues of meaning still remain,
As darkest myths meander through the pain
Towards a final formula of light.
I, too, reject that clarity of sight:
What cannot be explained, do not explain.

The mundane language of the senses sings
Its own interpretations. Common things
Become, by virtue of their commonness,
An argument against the nakedness
That dies of cold to find the truth it brings.

NIGHT OF THE SCORPION

I remember the night my mother
was stung by a scorpion. Ten hours
of steady rain had driven him
to crawl beneath a sack of rice.
Parting with his poison—flash
of diabolic tail in the dark room—
he risked the rain again.
The peasants came like swarms of flies
and buzzed the name of God a hundred times

to paralyze the Evil One.
With candles and with lanterns
throwing giant scorpion shadows
on the sun-baked walls
they searched for him: he was not found.
They clicked their tongues.
With every movement that the scorpion made
his poison moved in mother's blood, they said.
May he sit still, they said.
May the sins of your previous birth
be burned away tonight, they said.
May your suffering decrease
the misfortunes of your next birth, they said.
May the sum of evil
balanced in this unreal world
against the sum of good
become diminished by your pain, they said.
May the poison purify your flesh
of desire, and your spirit of ambition,
they said, and they sat around
on the floor with my mother in the centre,
the peace of understanding on each face.
More candles, more lanterns, more neighbours,
more insects, and the endless rain.
My mother twisted through and through
groaning on a mat.
My father, sceptic, rationalist,
trying every curse and blessing,
powder, mixture, herb and hybrid.
He even poured a little paraffin
upon the bitten toe and put a match to it.
I watched the flame feeding on my mother.
I watched the holy man perform his rites
to tame the poison with an incantation.
After twenty hours
it lost its sting.

My mother only said
Thank God the scorpion picked on me
and spared my children.

POET, LOVER, BIRDWATCHER

To force the pace and never to be still
Is not the way of those who study birds
Or women. The best poets wait for words.
The hunt is not an exercise of will
But patient love relaxing on a hill
To note the movement of a timid wing;
Until the one who knows that she is loved
No longer waits but risks surrendering—
In this the poet finds his moral proved,
Who never spoke before his spirit moved.

The slow movement seems, somehow, to say much more.
To watch the rarer birds, you have to go
Along deserted lanes and where the rivers flow
In silence near the source, or by a shore
Remote and thorny like the heart's dark floor.
And there the women slowly turn around,
Not only flesh and bone but myths of light
With darkness at the core, and sense is found
By poets lost in crooked, restless flight,
The deaf can hear, the blind recover sight.

THE VISITOR

Three times the crow has cawed
At the window, baleful eyes fixed
On mine, wings slightly raised
In sinister poise, body tense
And neck craned like a nagging woman's,
Filling the room with voice and presence.

Three times I got the message,
Sleep-walking on the air of thought
With muddy clothes, and floated down,

Concerned for all created things,
To cope with the visitor
Whose terms would compromise my own.

All day I waited, as befits
The folk belief that following
The crow a visitor would come,
An angel in disguise, perhaps,
Or else temptation in unlikely shape
To test my promises, ruin my sleep.

It was not like that at all.
His hands were empty, his need:
Only to kill a little time.
Between his good intentions
And my sympathy, the cigarette smoke
Was more substantial than our talk.

I see how wrong I was
Not to foresee precisely this:
Outside the miracles of mind,
The figure in the carpet blazing,
Ebb-flow of sex and the seasons,
The ordinariness of most events.

BACKGROUND, CASUALLY

1

A poet-rascal-clown was born,
The frightened child who would not eat
Or sleep, a boy of meagre bone.
He never learnt to fly a kite,
His borrowed top refused to spin.

I went to Roman Catholic school,
A mugging Jew among the wolves.
They told me I had killed the Christ,

That year I won the scripture prize.
A Muslim sportsman boxed my ears.

I grew in terror of the strong
But undernourished Hindu lads,
Their prepositions always wrong,
Repelled me by passivity.
One noisy day I used a knife.

At home on Friday nights, the prayers
Were said. My morals had declined.
I heard of Yoga and of Zen.
Could I, perhaps, be rabbi-saint?
The more I searched, the less I found.

Twenty-two: time to go abroad.
First, the decision, then a friend
To pay the fare. Philosophy,
Poverty and Poetry, three
Companions shared my basement room.

2

The London seasons passed me by.
I lay in bed two years alone,
And then a Woman came to tell
My willing ears I was the Son
Of Man. I knew that I had failed

In everything, a bitter thought.
So, in an English cargo-ship
Taking French guns and mortar-shells
To Indo-China, scrubbed the decks,
And learned to laugh again at home.

How to feel it home, was the point.
Some reading had been done, but what
Had I observed, except my own
Exasperation? All Hindus are
Like that, my father used to say,

When someone talked too loudly, or
Knocked at the door like the Devil.
They hawked and spat. They sprawled around.
I prepared for the worst. Married,
Changed jobs, and saw myself a fool.

The song of my experience sung,
I knew that all was yet to sing.
My ancestors, among the castes,
Were aliens crushing seed[1] for bread
(The hooded bullock made his rounds).

3

One among them fought and taught,
A Major bearing British arms.
He told my father sad stories
Of the Boer War. I dreamed that
Fierce men had bound my feet and hands.

The later dreams were all of words.
I did not know that words betray
But let the poems come, and lost
That grip on things the worldly prize.
I would not suffer that again.

I look about me now, and try
To formulate a plainer view:
The wise survive and serve—to play
The fool, to cash in on
The inner and the outer storms.

The Indian landscape sears my eyes.
I have become a part of it
To be observed by foreigners.
They say that I am singular.
Their letters overstate the case.

---

[1] Bene Israel tradition has it that their ancestors took to oil pressing soon after
their arrival in India. Hence, *shanwar teli*, Saturday oil-presser caste.

I have made my commitments now.
This is one: to stay where I am,
As others choose to give themselves
In some remote and backward place.
My backward place is where I am.

GOODBYE PARTY FOR MISS PUSHPA T. S.

Friends,
our dear sister
is departing for foreign
in two three days,
and
we are meeting today
to wish her bon voyage.

You are all knowing, friends,
what sweetness is in Miss Pushpa.
I don't mean only external sweetness
but internal sweetness.
Miss Pushpa is smiling and smiling
even for no reason
but simply because she is feeling.

Miss Pushpa is coming
from very high family.
Her father was renowned advocate
in Bulsar or Surat,
I am not remembering now which place.

Surat? Ah, yes,
once only I stayed in Surat
with family members
of my uncle's very old friend—
his wife was cooking nicely . . .
that was long time ago.

Coming back to Miss Pushpa
she is most popular lady
with men also and ladies also.

Whenever I asked her to do anything,
she was saying, 'Just now only
I will do it.' That is showing
good spirit. I am always
appreciating the good spirit.

Pushpa Miss is never saying no.
Whatever I or anybody is asking
she is always saying yes,
and today she is going
to improve her prospects
and we are wishing her bon voyage.

Now I ask other speakers to speak
and afterwards Miss Pushpa
will do the summing up.

POEM OF THE SEPARATION

To judge by memory alone,
our love was happy
when the bombs burst in Kashmir;
my life had burst
and merged in yours.

The war did not matter
though we tried to care,
the season, time and place
rejected their usual names.
One day you said,
'Suddenly, I feel
grown up.' The price was only
a thousand kisses.

Any man may be a whirlwind,
any woman lightning,
but buses take us to our meeting,
trains to our destination.
In these, and in cafés,
on beaches
and on benches in the park,
our music was made.

I ask you to pause
and to hear it again,
but you sweep ahead to hear
another music.
It's true we cannot live on echoes.

Ten thousand miles away,
you become a shower of letters,
a photograph, a newspaper cutting
underlined, with pencilled comments,
and a smell at night.

In the squalid, crude
city of my birth and rebirth,
you were a new way
of laughing at the truth.
I want you back
with the rough happiness you lightly wear,
supported by your shoulders,
breasts and thighs.

But you ask to break it up.
Your latest letter says:
'I am enclosing
Ramanujan's translation
of a Kannada religious poem:
"The Lord is playing
with streamers of fire."
I want to play with fire.
Let me get burnt.'

Arun Kolatkar

Arun Kolatkar was born in Kolhapur in 1932, and matriculated from Bombay University. He lives in Bombay, where he works in an advertising agency. His verse is, as yet, uncollected though some of it has appeared in *Opinion Literary Quarterly*, *An Anthology of Marathi Poetry* (Nirmala Sadanand Publishers, 1967), *New Writing in India* (Penguin Books, 1974) and *The Shell and the Rain* (George Allen and Unwin, 1973).

'the boatride' is characterized by a hypnotic stillness. Kolatkar's poetics is original, and it is in keeping with the incantatory quality of his experience. The absence of punctuation throughout reinforces this quality. The poem evokes a surreal world in which imagination and reality are fused, in which contradictions in logic are acceptable to the imagination, ordinary concepts of time and space do not operate, and everything is seen with an innocent eye.

'Jejuri' is a long poem in thirty-one sections, of which five are included here. Apparently it is about the poet's irreverent odyssey to the temple of Khandoba at Jejuri, a small town in western Maharashtra. In reality, however, the poem oscillates between faith and scepticism in a tradition that has run its course. Kolatkar expresses what he sees with the eye of a competent reporter in a language that is colloquial and spare. The result is a poem of unexpected beauty and power.

the boatride

the long hooked poles
know the nooks and crannies
find flaws in stonework
or grappling with granite
ignite a flutter
of unexpected pigeons
and the boat is jockeyed away from
the landing

after a pair of knees
has shot up and streaked
down the mast after
the confusion of hands about
the rigging

an off white miracle

the sail
      spreads

---

           because a sailor waved
                  back
to a boy

      another boy
waves to another sailor

in the clarity of air
the gesture withers for want
of correspondence and
the hand that returns to him
the hand his knee accepts
as his own
         is the hand
of an aged person
         a hand

that must remain patient
and give the boy it's a part of
time
      to catch up

---

frozen in a suit the foreman
self-conscious beside
his more self-conscious spouse
finds illegible the palm that opens
demandingly before him

the mould of his hands
broken about his right knee
he reaches for a plastic wallet
he pays the fares

along the rim of the boat
lightly the man rests his arm
without brushing against
his woman's shoulder

                gold
and sunlight
        fight
for the possession of her throat
when she shifts
in the wooden seat

and the newly weds exchange
smiles for small profit

---

show me a foreman he says
to himself
      who knows
his centreless grinding

oilfired saltbath furnace better
than i do
          and swears
at the seagull
who invents
on the spur of the air
what is clearly the whitest inflection
known
          and what is
clearly for the seagull
over and above the waves
a matter of course

---

the speedboat swerves off
leaving behind a divergence of sea
and the whole harbour all
that floats must bear
the briny brunt
the sailboat
hurl its hulk over
burly rollers
surmounted soon in leaps
and bounds

a gull hitched on hump
the long trail toils on
bringing to every craft
a measure of imbalance
a jolt for a dinghy
a fillip to a schooner
a swagger to a ketch

and after the sea wall
scabby and vicious with shells
has scalped the surge
after the backwash
has reverted to the bulk of water
all things that float

resume
a normal vacillation

---

winds bargaining over
his shrunken head
the mousy patriarch overgrown
with grandchildren
classifies a ship
first asserts and then proves
to the newest generation
that sea water
is salty
with the authority
of age you'll get
he tells the youngest
wet
    so putting in a nutshell
the dire consequence
of falling in water

the child cogitates
while the eyes of his
contemporaries
are already riveted
proudly to the portuguese ship they learn
the indians captured

---

his wife has dismissed
the waves like a queen
a band of oiled
acrobats

if her shuttered eyes
move in dark circles
they move against her will

winds
like the fingers
of an archaeologist
move across her stony face
and across the worn
edict of a smile
cut thereon

her husband in chains
is brought before her
he clanks and grovels

throw him to the wolves
she says
staring fixedly
at a hair in his right nostril

---

impatient with the surrounding gallons
of boredom spurning the rowdy
intangibles of waves
a two-year-old renounces
his mother's ear
and begins to cascade
down her person
rejecting her tattooed arm
denying her thighs
undaunted by her knees
and further down
her shanks
devolving
        he demands
              balloons
                  and balloons
from father to son
           are handed
           down

closer to keel than all
elders are

and down there
honoured among boots
chappals and bare feet
he goes into a huddle with
                    the balloons
                    coming to grips
with one
        being persuasive
with another
            and setting an example
            by punishing a third

---

two sisters
that came
last
when the boat
nearly started

seated side
by side
athwart
on a plank
have not
spoken

hands in lap
they have
been looking
past the boatman's
profile

splicing
the wrinkles
of his saline
face

and loose ends
of the sea

---

familiar perspectives
reoccupy
a cleanlier eye
sad as a century
the gateway of india
struggles back to its feet
wobbly but sober enough
to account for itself
details approach our memory
ingratiatingly
we are prepared to welcome
a more realistic sense
of proportion

a wind comes carrying
                              the microbe
of a melody

where the sea jostles
against the wall
vacuous sailboats snuggle
tall and gawky
their masts at variance
                    islam
                         mary
                              dolphin
their names appearing

                                        music
a black back turned
on all the waters of the arabic sea
a man plays on a *bulbul tarang*[1]
alone on the last boat
and facing the wall

---

the boat courses around
to sidle up

[1] Type of stringed instrument.

against the landing
the wall sweeps by
magisterially
superseding
the music man

an expanse of
unswerving stone
encrusted coarsely
with shells
admonishes our sight

---

from JEJURI[1]

THE BUS

The tarpaulin flaps are buttoned down
on the windows of the state transport bus
all the way up to Jejuri.

A cold wind keeps whipping
and slapping a corner of the tarpaulin
at your elbow.

You look down the roaring road.
You search for signs of daybreak in
what little light spills out of the bus.

Your own divided face in a pair of glasses
on an old man's nose
is all the countryside you get to see.

[1] Town 50 km south-east of Pune and sacred to Khandoba, an incarnation
of Siva.

You seem to move continually forward
towards a destination
just beyond the caste-mark between his eyebrows.

Outside, the sun has risen quietly.
It aims through an eyelet in the tarpaulin
and shoots at the old man's glasses.

A sawed-off sunbeam comes to a rest
gently against the driver's right temple.
The bus seems to change direction.

At the end of the bumpy ride
with your own face on either side
when you get off the bus

you don't step inside the old man's head.

AN OLD WOMAN

An old woman grabs
hold of your sleeve
and tags along.

She wants a fifty paise coin.
She says she will take you
to the horseshoe shrine.

You've seen it already.
She hobbles along anyway
and tightens her grip on your shirt.

She won't let you go.
You know how old women are.
They stick to you like burr.

You turn around and face her
with an air of finality.
You want to end the farce.

When you hear her say,
'What else can an old woman do
on hills as wretched as these?'

You look right at the sky.
Clear through the bullet holes
she has for her eyes.

And as you look on,
the cracks that begin around her eyes
spread beyond her skin.

And the hills crack.
And the temples crack.
And the sky falls

with a plateglass clatter
around the shatterproof crone
who stands alone.

And you are reduced
to so much small change
in her hand.

CHAITANYA[1]

'Sweet as grapes
are the stones of Jejuri,'
said Chaitanya.

He popped a stone
in his mouth
and spat out gods.

---

[1] Fifteenth-century Bengali saint whom some revere as an incarnation of Krishna.

MAKARAND

Take my shirt off
and go in there to do the puja?
No thanks.

Not me.
But you go right ahead
if that's what you want to do.

Give me the matchbox
before you go,
will you?

I will be out in the courtyard
where no one will mind it
if I smoke.

THE BLUE HORSE

The toothless singer
opens her mouth.
Shorts the circuits
in her haywire throat.
A shower of sparks
flies off her half-burnt tongue.

With a face fallen in on itself
and a black skin burnt blacker in the sun,
the drummer goes blue in the face
as he thumps and whacks the tambourine
and joins the chorus in a keyless passion.
His pockmarked half-brother
twiddles, tweaks and twangs
on the one-string thing.
God's own children
making music.

You turn to the priest
who has been good enough to arrange

5

that bit of sacred cabaret act at his own house
and ask him,
                    'The singers sang of a blue horse.
How is it then, that the picture on your wall
shows a white one?'
                              'Looks blue to me,'
says the priest,
shifting a piece of betel nut
from the left to the right of his mouth.
And draws an end of a nutcracker
along the underbelly of the noble animal.
Picking on a shade of blue
that many popular painters like to use
to suggest shadow on an object otherwise white.

The tambourine continues to beat its breast.

Shiv K. Kumar

Shiv Kumar Kumar was born in Lahore in 1921, and was educated at Dayanand Anglo-Vedic High School and Forman Christian College, Lahore and Fitzwilliam College, Cambridge. He lives in Hyderabad where he is Professor of English at the University of Hyderabad. He has been a Visiting Professor in several universities, including Cambridge and Yale. He toured Australia in 1971 as a Cultural Award Visitor. His works include *Articulate Silences* (1970), *Cobwebs in the Sun* (1974) and *The Last Wedding Anniversary* (1975), a play and *Subterfuges*, 1976. His poems have appeared in *Ariel* (Leeds), *Meanjin Quarterly* (Melbourne), *The New York Times*, *Quest* and *Western Humanities Review* (Salt Lake City).

Kumar brings a probing and alert mind to the situations of day-to-day living relieved by a rare ability to laugh at himself, as in 'Days in New York':

> Questions catapult in the air:
> 'Are you a Puerto Rican?
> A Jamaican? A Red Indian?'
> I look for the feathers on my skull,
> a band around my forehead.

One misses this pervasive, ironic humour in Indian verse in English generally. As he says, 'In view of my extensive travelling in the West, I seem to be constantly returning to the theme of cultural interaction. I feel, unconsciously, I guess, that with me contrast is almost a mode of perception. It is this awareness that compels me to recapture my days in New York as a kind of life-in-death.' Often he takes a simple fact or incident and develops it to a point where it acquires a new meaning. The poem about Indian women projects Kumar's response to a familiar situation: the impoverishment of the human spirit. Images of futility and hopelessness reinforce the structure of the poem. Here, nostalgia achieves the finish of an etching on copperplate.

INDIAN WOMEN

In this triple-baked continent
women don't etch angry eyebrows
on mud walls.
    Patiently they sit
    like empty pitchers
    on the mouth of the village well
pleating hope in each braid
of their mississippi-long hair
looking deep into the water's mirror
    for the moisture in their eyes.
    With zodiac doodlings on the sands
    they guard their tattooed thighs
waiting for their men's return
till even the shadows
roll up their contours
    and are gone
    beyond the hills.

MY CO-RESPONDENT

Not my rival but co-sharer,
your saliva is on my lips.
Often when she made the gesture
you were the prime mover.
    Just this difference though—
    while you rose like some giraffe
    I slouched over worms
    climbing up diamond-knots of wet grass.
    Each night I limped into my lone self
    where the dead croaked like frogs.
Now that I give you the rose to keep,
let me pass through the turnstile
into the open fields
where riderless horses whinny
under the red moon.

PILGRIMAGE

Not all of us spoke the same language—
some cowered under the sun's threats
and the dwindling supplies,
others felt amused
at the enforced equalities.
The bystanders took us for a Persian
mosaic of some insidious design.

Sometimes the urge to feign
was paramount. I pretended ataxia
to lag behind and visualize
more sharply the road's last, devious curve.

The trees on either side
would have given us a guard of honour
had our leader not defiled them
with blasphemies.

Then suddenly someone announced
that the easiest way to hit
the destination was to
march crabwise.

We were out to span the sky's amplitude—
this journey was merely to stimulate the blood.
The women mumbled, 'Rest would be haven—
indeed.'
I was the only one to caution
that the gods had trapped us
into belief.

DAYS IN NEW YORK[1]

Here I live in a garbage can.
The pile grows bigger each week
with the broken homes
splintered all around.
A black cat chases a shadow
down the passageway:
its whiskers presage another snowstorm.

The white of the negro maid's eyeballs
is the only clean thing here,
besides, of course, the quart gallon carton of milk
squatting at my door.
They wouldn't believe it here
that Ganges water can work miracles:
in spite of the cartloads
of dead men's ashes and bones—
daily offerings to the river.

I open each morning my neighbour's *Times*,
whisked away from his door
before he stirs.
Gloved hands leave no fingerprints.
And a brisk review of all our yesterdays is no sin.

En route to perdition
I sometimes stop at Grand Central to piss.
Where else can one ease one's nerves
when the bladder fills up
like a child's balloon?
In the Gents, each in his stall,
we stand reduced to the thing itself.
Questions catapult in the air:
'Are you a Puerto Rican?
A Jamaican? A Red Indian?'

---

[1] This is a revised version, the original of which appears in *Subterfuges* (Oxford University Press, 1976) as 'A Letter from New York'.

I look for the feathers on my skull,
a band around my forehead.
And mumble, 'No, a brown Indian,
from the land of Gandhi.'
The stranger briskly zips his soul
and vanishes past the shoeblack,
who turns to shine a lanky New Yorker
swaddled in the high chair like Lincoln.
Incidentally, there are no beggars at Grand Central.
Only eyes, eyes, eyes,
staring at lamp-posts.

Back in my den after dusk
I bandaid the day's bruises.
Outside the window perches the grey sky,
an ominous bird wrapped in nuclear fog.

At night the Voices of America
break in upon my tenuous frequency,
intoning the same fact three times,
till the sediment grips the Hudson's soul.
But my soul is still my own.
For, every Sunday morning, I descend
into purgatory,
the basement where three laundromats
gulp down nickels,
to wash all our sins.
But the brown of my skin defies
all bleachers.
How long will this eclipse last?

KALI[1]

Stone eyes of a mangled street dog
glare at my self's patina.
The rufous tongue of a cobra
sticks out each time
I circle round your ebony torso,
jabbed in the privates
by your devotees.

Beyond the priest's monotone
a lamb bleats for the knife-edge.
A child clinging to famished
nipples will die anyway,
but your nectar is the blood
that jets from fresh arteries.

If the way to create
is the way to kill,
I have hoarded enough blood
in my throat
for all the hyenas to suck from.

[1] Goddess of destruction to whom bloody sacrifices are offered.

Jayanta Mahapatra

Jayanta Mahapatra was born in Cuttack in 1928, and was educated at Stewart School and Ravenshaw College, Cuttack and Science College, Patna. He lives in Cuttack, where he is a Reader in Physics at Ravenshaw College. His works include *Close the Sky, Ten by Ten* (1971), *Svayamvara and Other Poems* (1971), *Countermeasures* (1973), poems translated from the Oriya of Soubhagya Misra and *A Rain of Rites* (1976). He has contributed to *Critical Quarterly* (Manchester), *The Malahat Review* (Victoria), *Meanjin Quarterly* (Melbourne), *Poetry* (Chicago) and *The Times Literary Supplement*. He was awarded the Jacob Glatstein Memorial Prize of *Poetry* (Chicago) in 1975.

Mahapatra explores the intricacies of human relationships, especially those of lovers, with a robust tenderness. About the poems themselves there is an unexpected quietude. He says, 'What appears to disturb me is the triumph of silence in the mind: and if these poems are inventions, they are also longings amid the flow of voices toward a need that I feel is defensive. A poem makes me see out of it in all directions, like a sieve, and I am almost relieved at that all-important thought.' Love offers a sort of relief from the uncertainties one has come to expect of life, probed rigorously, for instance, in 'Lost' and 'The Logic'. There is an intense, dramatic quality about 'A Missing Person'. The economy of phrasing and startling images recall the *subhāṣitas* (literally, that which is well said) of classical Sanskrit.

INDIAN SUMMER

Over the soughing of the sombre wind,
priests chant louder than ever:
the mouth of India opens.

Crocodiles move into deeper waters.

Mornings of heated middens
smoke under the sun.

The good wife
lies in my bed
through the long afternoon;
dreaming still, unexhausted
by the deep roar of funeral pyres.

A MISSING PERSON

In the darkened room
a woman
cannot find her reflection in the mirror

waiting as usual
at the edge of sleep.

In her hands she holds
the oil lamp
whose drunken yellow flames
know where her lonely body hides.

THE WHOREHOUSE IN A
CALCUTTA STREET

Walk right in. It is yours.
Where the house smiles wryly into the lighted street.
Think of the women
you wished to know and haven't.
The faces in the posters, the public hoardings.
And who are all *there* together,
those who put the house there
for the startled eye to fall upon,
where pasts join, and where they part.

The sacred hollow courtyard
that harbours the promise of a great conspiracy.
Yet nothing you do
makes a heresy of that house.
Are you ashamed to believe you're in this?
Then think of the secret moonlight of the women
left behind, their false chatter,
perhaps their reminding themselves
of looked-after children and of home:
the shooting stars in the eager darkness of return.

Dream children, dark, superfluous;
you miss them in the house's dark spaces, how can't you?
Even the women don't wear them—
like jewels or precious stones at the throat;
the faint feeling deep at a woman's centre
that brings back the discarded things:
the little turnings of blood
at the far edge of the rainbow.

You fall back against her in the dumb light,
trying to learn something more about women—
while she does what she thinks proper to please you,
the sweet, the little things, the imagined;
until the statue of the man within
you've believed in throughout the years

comes back to you, a disobeying toy—
and the walls you wanted to pull down,
mirror only of things mortal, and passing by:
like a girl holding on to your wide wilderness,
as though it were real, as though the renewing voice
tore the membrane of your half-woken mind
when, like a door, her words close behind:
'Hurry, will you? Let me go,'
and her lonely breath thrashed against your kind.

THE LOGIC

Recline in your upholstered chair
under the lemon-yellow logic,
in the golden corner of the light
clasping geometric hands together.
Point a finger, quote;
success, or something alike
construes you an accomplice.
Reviewing your cosy composed gesture
troglodytes had to find out,
you will not sleep with centuries
any more as with your women,
no more than you would
find me to be proof of you.
My skin cups unblemished milk
you shatter each lonely vein with,
my devoted pads of flesh pave the ground
for what you strove to accomplish.
Make me small and edible, love.
This scalp hurts not from the steep drag
of your hands but from my own practised drivel.

GRASS

Have I to negotiate it?
Moving slowly, sometimes throwing my great grief
across its shoulders, sometimes trailing it at my side,

I watch a little hymn
turning the ground beneath my feet,
a tolerant soil making its own way in the light of the sun.

It is just a mirror
marching away solemnly with me, lurching
into an ancestral smell of rot, reminding me

of secrets of my own:
the cracked earth of years, the roots staggering about
an impatient sensuality, bland heads heaving

in the loneliness of unknown winds.
Now I watch something out of the mind
scythe the grass, know that the trees end,

sensing the almost childlike submissiveness;
my hands that tear their familiar tormentors apart
waiting for their curse, the scabs of my dark dread.

LOST

Here I have learnt to recognize you
at a distance,
the evenings heavy,
the half-light wandering round the room.

I've wanted to know what lulling silence
can bloom in my hands,
what pain and pleasure your mind can wear
through the intrigues at my fingertips.

I watch your body ease off the seasons
stretched out on the stone of my breath,
going nowhere.

My hands move on.
Inside the lines on my moving palms,
is it time being sent back to somewhere far behind
on the edge of dream?
Is it that
which quietly shuts my eyes?

And outside my hands, where
your body keeps shrinking in space,
the first faith of some child goes wrong
like some defect in a mechanical toy;
yet what does it lead to?
To what fateful encounter?

Like a misplaced watch, this half-light.
Where was I when I lost it?

Arvind Krishna Mehrotra

Arvind Krishna Mehrotra was born in Lahore in 1947, and was educated at the Universities of Allahabad and Bombay. He lives in Allahabad where he is a Lecturer in English Literature at the University. His works include *Bharatmata: A Prayer* (1966), *Woodcuts on Paper* (1967), *Pomes/Poems/Poemas* (1971) and *Three* (1973), poems translated from the Macedonian of Bogomil Gjuzel. During 1971–3, he was a member of the University of Iowa's International Writing Program, and in Summer 1972 he was in residence at Yaddo, Saratoga Springs, New York. From 1965 to 1968 he was co-editor of *damn you / a magazine of the arts*. A year later, he founded a small literary press, Ezra-Fakir. He has had poems published in *The American Review* (New York), *Modern Poetry in Translation* (London), *The New York Quarterly* and *New Writing in India* (Penguin Books, 1974).

Mehrotra cites *Manifesto of Surrealism* (1924) as one of the influences on his work. This explains his addiction to the 'immoderate and passionate use of the drug which is the image'. He uses images in a subtle, insinuating manner that transfigures what he writes, often at the expense of logial coherence. 'The Sale' exemplifies this characteristic to an unusual degree. Here, the jargon of a sales chat acquires a lyrical intensity as images are piled one on top of another in defiance of common sense:

> You remember in my letter
> I wrote of forests? they're wrapped
> in leaves and there should be
> no trouble in carrying them. . . .
> I must also show you a tiger's skin
> which once hid a palace.

As Mehrotra explains, a poem comprises 'games, riddles and accidents . . . and the poet creates as many accidents as he can'.

THE SALE

1

It's yours for the price, and these
old bits have character too. Today
they may not be available.
Naturally I can't press you
to buy them, and were I not leaving—
you hear the sun choking with an eclipse—
I would never have thought of selling.
You may take your time though, and
satisfy yourself. Yes, this is Europe,
that America. This scarecrow Asia,
that groin Africa and amputated
Australia. These five, I don't have more.
Maybe another egg-laying island remains
in the sea. You remember in my letter
I wrote of forests? They're wrapped
in leaves and there should be
no trouble in carrying them.
This skull contains the rivers.
Of that I'm sorry. Had you come
yesterday I might have given you two.
I shall take another look. Yes, I do
have a mummy somewhere; only last
night the pyramids came
and knocked at my gate for a long time.

2

Would you mind if I showed you
a few more things now yours?
Be careful, one river is still wet
and slippery; its waters continue to
run like footprints. Well, this is a
brick and we call that string.
This microscope contains the margins
of a poem. I have a map left, drawn
by migrating birds.

Come into the attic.
That's not a doll—it's the
photograph of a brain walking
on sand and in the next one
it's wearing an oasis-like crown.
I must also show you a tiger's skin
which once hid a palace.
On one roof you'll see
the antelope's horns,
on another the falling wind. These round
things are bangles and that long one
a gun. This cave is the inside
of a boot. And here
carved wheels turn through stone.

3

I wish you had asked me earlier.
The paintings have been bought
by a broken mirror
but I think I can lead you
to a crack in the wall.
I've a skeleton too.
It's full of butterflies
who at dawn will carry away
the crown.
I've also a wheel-chair to show you;
it belonged to my uncle
and one day the hook
which hangs from the sky
touched him. If you open the
cupboard you'll see his memory
on the upper shelves and two books
now yours.
Ruskin's *Lectures on Art* and
A Short History of English Literature by Legouis.
I'll take another minute.
Can you climb this ladder?
Well, that's the sun and moon
and with this candle you can

work the clouds. I'm sorry I was
short of space
and had to pack the Great Bear
in this clock. Oh them,
let them not worry you.
They're only fisherman and king
who will sail soon as one's bait
is ready and the other's dominion.

CONTINUITIES

1

This is about the green miraculous trees
And old clocks on stone towers
And playgrounds full of light
And dark blue uniforms.
At eight I am a boy scout and make a tent
By stretching a bedsheet over parallel bars
And a fire by burning rose bushes.
I know half a dozen knots and imagine
Tea in enamel mugs.
I wear khaki knickers, take down
The number plates of cars
Make a perfect about turn for the first time.
In September I collect my cousins' books
And find out the dates of the six Mugals
To secretly write the history of India.
I see Napoleon crossing the Alps
On a white horse.

2

My first watch is a fat and silver Omega
Grandfather won in a race fifty-nine years ago.
It never works and I have to
Push its hands every few minutes

To get a clearer picture of time.
Somewhere I have kept my autograph book
The tincture of iodine in homeopathy bottles
Bright postcards he sent from
Bad Ems, Germany.
At seven thirty we are sent home
From the Cosmopolitan Club.
My father says, 'No bid,'
My mother forgets her hand
In a deck of cards.
I sit on the railing till midnight
Above a worn sign
That advertises a dentist.

3

I go to sleep after I hear him
Snore like the school bell.
I am standing alone in a back alley
And a face I can never recollect is removing
The hub caps from our dull brown Ford.
The first words I mumble are the names of roads,
Colvin, Clive and Lytton.
We live in a small cottage:
I grow up on a guava tree
Wondering where the servants vanish
After dinner; at the magic of the bearded tailor
Who can change the shape of my ancestors.
I bend down from the swaying bridge
And pick up the river
Which once tried to hide me.
The dance of the torn skin
Is for much later.

A LETTER TO A FRIEND

I set up house while she waited
In another city; the day of our marriage
Was still far. When she saw the rooms
For the first time she said,
'These are worse than bathrooms.'
She found the walls too narrow and wanted
To run away; your mother and my aunt
Were both there when this happened.
Your mother, in her enthusiasm
And simple joy
Asked us over to lunch
When she said, 'I know nothing of lunches.'
It was months before things got normal again.
Anyhow, she spent her first days
With the clear sky, a few birds.
The little interesting things that gather
Around trees; we slept in the afternoon
And awoke when the long, sad evening
Was already half-way up the window.
Kitchen smoke, the quiet smell
Of me reading in my chair,
The glum books that smacked their tails
Upon the shelves like field mice,
The family downstairs quarrelling and crying
Poisoned the tips of needles in her mind
And she entered an imprisoned kingdom,
A place I wouldn't touch with my bare hands.
Through two short rooms she walked
As if I were out to murder her last secret
And a blackness we all feel took hold of me.
I wanted it to, to protect myself;
Her eyes glistened, scared, scary.
At night insects on wings and feet would come
To relieve the stiff air.
We all played under the sharp moon
Making little noise for I barely touched her.
The first caw and the excitement

Of crows as they looked at us in bed from the chimney.
Bees rushed into the room with
Horns, bells, whistles.
The sun pulled up
And the girl next door wrung her underwear.
She knew I admired her ankles even in sleep.
The milkwoman brought her dog with her,
The postman came up the steps and she spent
Hours reading letters from her family,
Then replied to each one of her brothers and sisters.
The lama would knock and take off his shoes
Before entering; he'd hold her hand and talk
Of silence, of living in the mountains
With just enough candles to scatter the dark.
We fetched water in heavy buckets
Cooked in the open
And lying on the hillside none thought of love.
She made tea by boiling
The leaves, water, milk and sugar
Together, adding condiments at the end.
When he left her palms were wet
And I wasn't jealous.
Across the clean, flat roofs and narrow road
Is a bare field; a camel once sat there all day,
Thin legs folded under the hump,
Looking at cows walk through the trees.
So has it been.
Her blood has got more entangled in its stones
While I've kept to my lamp, beads, mirrors, jars,
A rug, pictures of purple demons,
Red, black and white ants, all sorts of fat spiders.
Three years, and I still wonder
What nakedness is, or does.
Sometimes I notice the couple next door.
It's very warm outside
And the streets
                    are tall and quiet.

REMARKS OF AN EARLY
BIOGRAPHER

1

There was something there we did
Not know before, that he hadn't
Mentioned in rhyme; our first job
Was to coax the ancient vase
Into letting us enter.
The dust hung in mid air.
The books he hadn't finished
Lived and waited in the walls.
The desk, when it saw us, raised
The drawbridge.
In all we spent three days
Expecting some bird, some omen
To turn up another secret.
We came down the steps
Remembering we hadn't climbed them
To get there; we looked back
And the room had folded.

2

Then one summer day
Just as the sun rose on its thin
Elbows I returned, alone.
The lines in my pocket bore
A resemblance to ivory knives
And kept the fresh smell of gunpowder.
On pane and mirror
I interpreted the shapes of light
And uncovered the route he took
To escape into the clean
Edges of the sky.
The river had aged, becoming
A serpent with invisible scales.
The old banyan tree slept,
Its head filled with roots.

The women of that city asked,
'Has he opened or shut the windows?'

3

In his keen memory he stored
His silences like mistresses
And it isn't my intention
To disturb that symmetry of holes.
As I turn the pages of his notebook
A few characters come apart;
I once more prod
The shallow vessel filled with ash
Then return my guides to their frontiers
The spider to the trellis
The rat to the cupboard
The lizard to the brick.
As a child he divided words
With a blade, or turned them
Inside out like caps; at death
His mouth was open, his right hand warm
As if it had never written.

R. Parthasarathy

Rajagopal Parthasarathy was born at Tirupparaiturai near Tiruch-chirappalli in 1934, and was educated at Don Bosco High School and Siddharth College, Bombay and Leeds University, where he was a British Council Scholar in 1963–4. He was a Lecturer in English Literature in Bombay for ten years. In 1971 he moved to Madras as Regional Editor, Oxford University Press. His works include *Poetry from Leeds* (1968), which he edited with J. J. Healy, and *Rough Passage* (1976). He has had poems published in *Encounter*, *London Magazine*, *Poetry India*, *Quest* and *The Times Literary Supplement*. He was awarded the Ulka Poetry Prize of *Poetry India* in 1966.

'Exile', 'Trial' and 'Homecoming', each represented here by a few sections, together form the three parts of *Rough Passage*, a long poem written over a period of fifteen years between 1961 and 1975 in which Parthasarathy dwells upon the question of language and identity and upon the inner conflict that arises from being brought up in two cultures. 'Exile', the first part, opposes the culture of Europe with that of India, and examines the consequences of British rule on an Indian, especially the loss of identity with his own culture and there-fore the need for roots. Against the turmoil of non-relationship, personal love holds forth the promise of belonging, and the second part, 'Trial', celebrates love as a reality here and now. 'Homecoming', the third and final part of *Rough Passage*, explores the phenomenon of returning to one's home. It is a sort of overture made with the aim of starting a dialogue between the poet and his Tamil past. The strength of the poem derives from his sense of responsibility towards crucial personal events in his life.

from EXILE

2

Through holes in a wall, as it were,
lamps burned in the fog.
In a basement flat, conversation

filled the night, while Ravi Shankar,
cigarette stubs, empty bottles of stout
and crisps provided the necessary pauses.

He had spent his youth whoring
after English gods.
There is something to be said for exile:

you learn roots are deep.
That language is a tree, loses colour
under another sky.

The bark disappears with the snow,
and branches become hoarse.
However, the most reassuring thing

about the past is that it happened.
Dressed in tweeds or grey flannel,
its suburban pockets

bursting with immigrants—
'coloureds' is what they calls us
over there—the city is no jewel, either:

lanes full of smoke and litter,
with puddles of unwashed
English children.

On New Year's Eve he heard an old man
at Trafalgar Square, 'It's no use trying
to change people. They'll be what they are.

An empire's last words are heard
on the hot sands of Africa.
The da Gamas, Clives, Dupleixs are back.

Victoria sleeps on her island
alone, an old hag,
shaking her invincible locks.'

Standing on Westminster Bridge,
it seemed the Thames had clogged
the chariot wheels of Boadicea to a stone.

Under the shadow of poplars
the river divides the city from the night.
The noises reappear,

of early trains, the milkman,
and the events of the day become
vocal in the newsboy.

8

A grey sky oppresses the eyes:
porters, rickshaw-pullers, barbers, hawkers,
fortune-tellers, loungers compose the scene.

Above them towers the bridge,
a pale diamond in the water.
Trees, big with shade, squat in the maidan

as I walk, my tongue hunchbacked
with words, towards Jadavpur
to your arms. You smell of gin

and cigarette ash. Your breasts,
sharp with desire, hurt my fingers.
Feelings beggar description,

shiver in dark alleys of the mind,
hungry and alone. Nothing can really
be dispensed with. The heart needs all.

The years have given me little wisdom,
and I've dislodged myself to find it.
Here, on the banks of the Hooghly,

in the city Job Charnock[1] built.
I shall carry this wisdom to another city
in the bone urn of my mind.

These ashes are all that's left
of the flesh and brightness of youth.
My life has come full circle: I'm thirty.

I must give quality to the other half.
I've forfeited the embarrassing gift
innocence in my scramble to be man.

from TRIAL

1

Mortal as I am, I face the end
with unspeakable relief,
knowing how I should feel

if I were stopped and cut off.
Were I to clutch at the air,
straw in my extremity,

how should I not scream,
'I haven't finished?'
Yet that too would pass unheeded.

Love, I haven't the key
to unlock His gates.
Night curves.

[1] Agent of the East India Company's station at Hooghly and founder of Calcutta.

I grasp your hand
in a rainbow of touch. Of the dead
I speak nothing but good.

2

Over the family album, the other night,
I shared your childhood:
the unruly hair silenced by bobpins

and ribbons, eyes half-shut
before the fierce glass,
a ripple of arms round Suneeti's neck,

and in the distance, squatting
on fabulous haunches
of all things, the Taj.

School was a pretty kettle of fish:
the spoonfuls of English
brew never quite slaked your thirst.

Hand on chin, you grew up,
all agog, on the cook's succulent
folklore. You rolled yourself

into a ball the afternoon Father died,
till time unfurled you
like a peal of bells. How your face

bronzed, as flesh and bone struck
a touchwood day. Purged,
you turned the corner in a child's steps.

7

It is night alone helps
to achieve a lucid exclusiveness.
Time that had dimmed

your singular form
by its harsh light now makes
recognition possible

through this opaque lens.
Touch brings the body into focus,
restores colour to inert hands,

till the skin takes over,
erasing angularities, and the four walls
turn on a strand of hair.

9

A knock on the door:
you entered.
Undressed quietly before the mirror

of my hands. Eyes
drowned in the skull
as flesh hardened to stone.

I have put aside the past
in a corner, an umbrella
now poor in the ribs. The touch

of your breasts is ripe
in my arms. They obliterate my eyes
with their tight parabolas of gold.

It's you I commemorate tonight.
The sweet water
of your flesh I draw

with my arms, as from a well,
its taste as ever
as on the night of Capricorn.

It's two in the morning:
my thoughts turn to you. With lamp
and pen I blow the dust off my past.

Come in, and see for yourself.
It's taken thirty odd years.
Now, a small hand will do.

10

It was the August heat
brought the stars to a boil,
and you asked me about constellations.

Yet, by itself, your hand was a galaxy
I could reach, even touch
in the sand with my half-inch telescopic

fingers. Overwhelm the flight
of human speech. Thus celebrate
something so perishable, trite.

from HOMECOMING

1

My tongue in English chains,
I return, after a generation, to you.
I am at the end

of my dravidic tether,
hunger for you unassuaged.
I falter, stumble.

Speak a tired language
wrenched from its sleep in the *Kural*,[1]
teeth, palate, lips still new

to its agglutinative touch.
Now, hooked on celluloid, you reel
down plush corridors.

[1] Tamil classic of the third or fourth century A.D. by Valluvar.

3

And so it eventually happened—
a family reunion not heard of
since grandfather died in '59—in March

this year. Cousins arrived in Tiruchchanur
in overcrowded private buses,
the dust of unlettered years

clouding instant recognition.
Later, each one pulled,
sitting crosslegged on the steps

of the choultry,[1] familiar coconuts
out of the fire
of rice-and-pickle afternoons.

Sundari, who had squirrelled up and down
forbidden tamarind trees in her long skirt
every morning with me,

stood there, that day, forty years taller,
her three daughters floating
like safe planets near her.

4

I made myself an expert
in farewells. An unexpected November
shut the door in my face:

I crashed, a glasshouse
hit by the stone of Father's death.
At the burning ghat

relations stood like exclamation points.
The fire stripped his unwary body
of the last shred of family likeness.

[1] Inn.

I am my father now.
The lines of my hands
hold the fine compass of his going:

I shall follow. And after me,
my unborn son, through the eye of this needle
of forgetfulness.

8

With paper boats boys tickle her ribs,
and buffalos have turned her to a pond.
There's eaglewood in her hair

and stale flowers. Every evening,
as bells roll in the forehead of temples,
I see a man on the steps

clean his arse. Kingfishers and egrets,
whom she fed, have flown
her paps. Also emperors and poets

who slept in her arms. She is become
a sewer, now. No one has any use for Vaikai,
river, once, of this sweet city.

10

The street in the evening tilts homeward
as traffic piles up.
It is then I stir about.

Rise from the table and shake the dust
from my eyes. Pick up
my glasses and look for myself

in every nook and corner
of the night. The pavement turns informer
hearing my steps. A pariah dog

slams an alley in my face.
I have exchanged the world
for a table and chair. I shouldn't complain.

12

I see him now sitting at his desk.
The door is open. It is evening.
On the lawns the children play.

He went for the wrong gods from the start.
And marriage made it worse.
He hadn't read his Greek poets well:

better to bury a woman than marry her.
Now he teaches. Reviews verse
written by others. Is invited to conferences

and attends them. How long it had taken
him to learn he had no talent
at all, although words came easy.

One can be articulate about nothing.
Or, was it simply
his god had left him?

Pedalling his bicycle glasses, he asks,
'What's it like to be a poet?'
I say to myself, 'The son of a bitch

fattens himself on the flesh of dead poets.
Lines his pockets with their blood.
From his fingertips ooze ink and paper,

as he squats on the dungheap
of old texts and obscure commentaries.
His eyes peal off.

Where would His Eminence be
but for the poets who splashed about
in the Hellespont or burned in the Java Sea?'

14

I am no longer myself as I watch
the evening blur the traffic
to a pair of obese headlights.

I return home, tired,
my face pressed against the window
of expectation. I climb the steps

to my flat, only to trip over the mat
outside the door. The key
goes to sleep in my palm.

I fear I have bungled again.
That last refinement of speech
terrifies me. The balloon

of poetry has grown red in the face
with repeated blowing. For scriptures
I, therefore, recommend

the humble newspaper: I find
my prayers occasionally answered there.
I shall, perhaps, go on

like this, unmindful of day
melting into the night.
My heart I have turned inside out.

Hereafter, I should be content,
I think, to go through life
with the small change of uncertainties.

Gieve Patel

Gieve Patel was born in Bombay in 1940, and was educated at St Xavier's High School and Grant Medical College. He lives in Bombay where he is a general practitioner. His works include *Poems* (1966) and *Princes*, a play performed in 1970 by the Theatre Group and so far unpublished. His poems have appeared in *The Illustrated Weekly of India*, *New Writing in India* (Penguin Books, 1974) and *Young Commonwealth Poets '65* (Heinemann, 1965).

Patel's poems are unspectacular take-offs on the Indian scene on which he comments with clinical fastidiousness. This accounts for his dead-pan tone and sparse use of images. In 'Naryal Purnima', the Hindu festival provides him, a Parsi, with an occasion to diagnose his own attitudes in the hope of knowing himself better as a human being. His sympathies are with the oppressed, the underdog—anyone denied the right to live. The peroration is visually impressive, and humour comes to the poet's rescue as he resolves the conflict within himself. Patel believes that 'if a poem is clear, well thought out, purposive, logical and true, it will have changed something . . . first, in the poet himself . . . because if this does not happen . . . there is no poem'. His poems rightly, therefore, try to make articulate, often sardonically, the pains of growing up.

ON KILLING A TREE

It takes much time to kill a tree,
Not a simple jab of the knife
Will do it. It has grown
Slowly consuming the earth,
Rising out of it, feeding
Upon its crust, absorbing
Years of sunlight, air, water,
And out of its leprous hide
Sprouting leaves.

So hack and chop
But this alone won't do it.
Not so much pain will do it.
The bleeding bark will heal
And from close to the ground
Will rise curled green twigs,
Miniature boughs
Which if unchecked will expand again
To former size.

No,
The root is to be pulled out—
Out of the anchoring earth;
It is to be roped, tied,
And pulled out—snapped out
Or pulled out entirely,
Out from the earth-cave,
And the strength of the tree exposed,
The source, white and wet,
The most sensitive, hidden
For years inside the earth.

Then the matter
Of scorching and choking
In sun and air,
Browning, hardening,
Twisting, withering,

And then it is done.

SERVANTS

They come of peasant stock,
Truant from an insufficient plot.

Lights are shut off after dinner
But the city-blur enters,
Picks modulations on the skin;
The dark around them
Is brown, and links body to body,
Or is dispelled, and the hard fingers
Glow as smoke is inhaled
And the lighted end of tobacco
Becomes an orange spot.

Other hands are wide
Or shut, it does not matter
One way or other—
They sit without thought,
Mouth slightly open, recovering
From the day, and the eyes
Globe into the dim
But are not informed because
Never have travelled beyond this
Silence. They sit like animals.
I mean no offence. I have seen
Animals resting in their stall,
The oil flame reflected in their eyes,
Large beads that though protruding
Actually rest
Behind the regular grind
Of the jaws.

NARGOL

This time you did not come
To trouble me. I left the bus
Wiping dust from my lashes
And did not meet you all the way
Home. At the back of my mind,
Behind greetings, dog-licks, and deepening
Safety, I continued to look for you—
But my strolls continued pleasant—
I did not spot you at the end of a lane,
Your necklace pendulant as your skin,
Your cringing smile pointing the disease:
Leper-face, leonine, following my elbow
As I walk past casual, casual.
I am friendly, I smile, I am
No snob. Lepers don't disgust me. But also
Tough resistance: I have no money,
Meet me later,
My fingernail rasping a coin.
She'll have her money but
Cannot be allowed to bully—
Let her follow, let her drone,
Sooner or later she'll give up,
Stop in the centre of a lane,
Let herself recede.
I reach the sea.
Yes, that was essential.
Discipline.

In the open street I stand
With elders. How far have you
Studied, when do you finish?
In the middle of my reply
She passes by,
I skip a word, she cannot
Meet my eye, grins timidly, goes on;
Accepted fact
This is not the time.

Afternoon, and she reappears,
Stands before the house, says
Nothing, looks for my eyes
Between page-turns. I cannot read.
The book is frozen, angry weapon
In my hand. I pretend a page,
Then look up—I'm reading now I say,
I'll give you later—switch down,
Master, unquestioned. She goes.

Cruel, you're cruel.

From a village full of people
She has chosen me; year after year;
Is it need
Or a private battle?

At the end it is four annas[1]—
Four annas for leprosy. It's green
To give so much
But I am a rich man's son.
She cringes—I've worked for your mother.
She hasn't—
You come just once a year.
All right, a rupee. She goes.
My strolls are to myself again,
The sea is reached with ease,
Reading is simplified. One last tussle:
Was it not defeat after all?
Personal, since I did not give,
I gave in; wider—there was
No victory even had I given.
I have lost to a power too careless
And sprawling to admit battle,
And meanness no defence.
Walking to the sea I carry
A village, a city, the country,
For the moment
On my back.

---

[1] Former copper coin, a sixteenth part of a rupee.

This time you did not come
To trouble me. In the middle
Of a lane I stopped.
She's dead, I thought;
And after relief, the next thought:
She'll reappear
If only to baffle.

NARYAL PURNIMA[1]
(August 1965)

1

They say the seas change mood today,
Pronounce an official end to the rains—
And this year they did—the generous
Curtain shrank upward
For once according to the calendar
To ignore our need: a month
Of deluge and then these brilliant
Beautiful days of drought.
Naryal Purnima should be a few days' halt
Before the second rains begin; the rice
Sprouted, transplanted, yet doomed to die
Without a new month's grace of extra water.

The first rains bore fruit, I'm told.
The country pushed root, prepared to fling
An arc of branches; yet I know nothing today
Of feeling or intellect that condensed to form
Nineteenth-century grain.
Only a faded haze remains
Over academic portraits in public buildings:
Gentle beards a trifle unreal, patriotic songs

[1] Hindu festival held at full moon during August–September when the sea-god
Varuna is propitiated with coconuts to mark the end of the monsoon. Also called
Coconut Day.

And as Chaudhuri[1] explains,
A well-meaning spider weaving us
Into a maze. The disciple turned once
To share a joke. A camera clicked. And
Our calendars repeat the image to exhaustion,
Reaching perhaps
For the ambiguous implication.

2

Marine Drive is sharp. I can see
Each wavelet like a chip of cut-glass and
Almost all the leaves on Malabar Hill. I sit,
Non-conformist, facing the sea, my back set
To the rich and the less rich as they come
Scrubbed and bathed, carrying a dirty little satchel
With a nut for the gods. Had I the will to trouble
I'd be with the others—the driftwood
From the South, poised black and lean
Against a blinking sea—
Their minds profanely focused
On the wave-pitched gifts.
Do I sympathize merely with the underdog?
Is it one more halt in the search for 'identity'?

Our interiors never could remain
Quite English. The local gods hidden in
Cupboards from rational Parsi eyes
Would suddenly turn up on the walls
Garlanded alongside the King and the Queen.
And the rulers who had such praise for our manners
Disappeared one day. So look instead for something else:
Even accept and belong. Grit teeth and recite:
'This is the poet's land. The sun's blinding life,
The ear-splitting pipes penetrate the soul.
The petty glare may be counterpart.
The round rain-clouds, the soft thick thunder,

---

[1] In *The Autobiography of an Unknown Indian,* Nirad C. Chaudhuri refers to Gandhi as a 'well-meaning spider'.

Set loose the fat and the oil. Love one
Love the other.' But there's effort involved.
Today it is simpler to admit with relief:
'The men are too greasy, their speech
Is too nasal, their wives either plain
Or overdone; they choose for their dresses
A shattering blue and choke their flowers
In tinsel; their mind is provincial,
Their children are dull.' And a relief to turn
From these suppliants to the urchins,
Their meagre flesh etching a problem
Perhaps not of the mind, their hunger present
As common factor, ground of dark rest
From twenty doubts, indisputable birth-mark
To recognize
Myself and the country by.
For a moment I forget to think:
'Eternally ignorant, stranded through ages,
Pesky beggars unwilling to work,
Their language a pointless gargle,
Their skin dirty and dark.'

Hear me instead apostrophize:
'As you stand half-naked on the walls
And wait for coconuts to strike the sea,
And pose intent and ready to dive in
Before they be borne too far out of reach,
There could be cynicism at least
On your faces, if not accusation, as I sit
Casual commentor, but surely not this
Innocuous smile at my interest?'

The urchins strip to plunge.
The oily ones are startled. The men
Look flustered, imperiously order them
Away; the women squawk in their sharp
Brittle clothes. But the drifters stay:
As coconuts are tossed and touch water
My present identities dive, snatch libations
From under god's nose.

The rains may truly fail this year.
Our prayers may go unheard.

COMMERCE

I force initially simplicity of commerce,
A rupee note changes hands.
His tongue is loosened, and squatting by me,
Straightening the groundspread, his
Offered hospitality, he talks.
I anticipate defeat, feel cheated from the start.
These, as usual, will be external gestures.
As always, what is unexpressed will roll
Darkly behind his eyes and click shut.
Yet I listen again.
Unmistakable the difference.
It is he searching me out.
Enquiries after my job or family
Not a screen this time for the quietly guarded.
I would seek to escape the challenge he poses.
Simple enough his look. Wife and child
At the rear of the hut penetrate
The darkness cocoon, endorse
The man's enquiries. This
May well happen again, I tell myself.
Permitting my mouth I might spark into speech.
What then, Sir Poet, of political choices?

O MY VERY OWN CADAVER

I see my body float on waters
That rush down the street,
Like a leaf that humps its way
Over pebbles. To be so reduced

To flatness like a translucent
Cellophane doll, insubstantial,
Dented by passing feet, but
Tough as plastics!
I think a body may with ease meet
A less bizarre fate
Though I won't willingly forgo
This one. The things this body would do
When cut off at last from breathing!
Brazenly it plans competitions
With the living. If merrily
It condescends to slide
Over moss, see in it a
Calculation. Of various forms
It might have chosen, flatness
Is what it wants. As my cellophane self
Grinds and drags against rushing
Water, watch the kicking,
The shivering. Now who would suspect
The inch to square
Inch cuticular ecstasies
Of this shameless carnal?

A. K. Ramanujan

Attippat Krishnaswami Ramanujan was born in Mysore in 1929, and was educated at D. Bhanumaiah's High School and Maharaja's College, Mysore. He was a fellow of Deccan College, Poona in 1958–59 and a Fulbright Scholar at Indiana University in 1960–62. He was a Lecturer in English Literature in Quilon, Belgaum and Baroda for eight years. Since 1962, he has been at the University of Chicago, where he is now Professor of Dravidian Studies and Linguistics. His works include *Fifteen Tamil Poems* (1965), *The Striders* (1966), *The Interior Landscape* (1967), *No Lotus in the Navel* (1969), *Relations* (1971) and *Speaking of Siva* (1972) and *Selected Poems* (1976). *The Striders* was a Poetry Society Recommendation. He was awarded the Gold Medal of the Tamil Writers Association for *The Interior Landscape* in 1969. He has contributed to *The Atlantic Monthly, London Magazine, Poetry* (Chicago), *Quest* and *The Penguin Book of Love Poems* (Penguin Books, 1974).

For the past fifteen years, he has lived in the United States. His Indian experience repeatedly features in his verse, and is often precisely recreated in its original setting. But his American experience seems less frequently to impinge on his verse or, for that matter, round off anomalies in his obviously Hindu outlook. India and America tend to exist separately, and come together, however, only at a time of personal crisis explored, for instance, in 'Still Another View of Grace'.

He has an eye for the specific physiognomy of an object or situation which he then reveals with telling detail, as in the luminous evocations of his family life in the poems collected in *Relations*, particularly 'Small-scale Reflections on a Great House', 'Love Poem to a Wife 1' and 'Of Mothers, among Other Things'. The family, for Ramanujan, is in fact one of the central metaphors with which he thinks.

'A River' is a poem on the Vaikai which flows through Madurai, a city that has for about two thousand years been the seat of Tamil culture. As an evocation of a river the poem succeeds admirably. At the same time, the river becomes a point of departure for ironically contrasting the relative attitudes of the old and new Tamil poets, both of whom are exposed for their callousness to suffering, when it is so obvious, as a result of the floods.

Ramanujan writes, 'English and my disciplines (linguistics, anthropology) give me my "outer" forms—linguistic, metrical, logical and other such ways of shaping experience; and my first thirty years in India, my frequent visits and fieldtrips, my personal and professional preoccupations with Kannada, Tamil, the classics and folklore give me my substance, my "inner" forms, images and symbols. They are continuous with each other, and I no longer can tell what comes from where.'

His poems are like the patterns in a kaleidoscope, and every time he turns it around one way or other, to observe them more closely, the results never fail to astonish.

LOOKING FOR A COUSIN
ON A SWING

When she was four or five
she sat on a village swing
and her cousin, six or seven,
sat himself against her;
with every lunge of the swing
she felt him
in the lunging pits
of her feeling;
    and afterwards
we climbed a tree, she said,

not very tall, but full of leaves
like those of a fig tree,

and we were very innocent
about it.

Now she looks for the swing
in cities with fifteen suburbs
and tries to be innocent
about it

not only on the crotch of a tree
that looked as if it would burst
under every leaf
into a brood of scarlet figs

if someone suddenly sneezed.

A RIVER

In Madurai,
        city of temples and poets
who sang of cities and temples:

every summer
a river dries to a trickle
in the sand,
baring the sand-ribs,
straw and women's hair
clogging the watergates
at the rusty bars
under the bridges with patches
of repair all over them,
the wet stones glistening like sleepy
crocodiles, the dry ones
shaven water-buffalos lounging in the sun.

The poets sang only of the floods.

He was there for a day
when they had the floods.
People everywhere talked
of the inches rising,
of the precise number of cobbled steps
run over by the water, rising
on the bathing places,
and the way it carried off three village houses,
one pregnant woman
and a couple of cows
named Gopi and Brinda, as usual.

The new poets still quoted
the old poets, but no one spoke
in verse
of the pregnant woman
drowned, with perhaps twins in her,
kicking at blank walls
even before birth.

He said:
the river has water enough
to be poetic
about only once a year
and then
it carries away
in the first half-hour
three village houses,
a couple of cows
named Gopi and Brinda
and one pregnant woman
expecting identical twins
with no moles on their bodies,
with different-coloured diapers

to tell them apart.

OF MOTHERS, AMONG
OTHER THINGS

I smell upon this twisted
blackbone tree the silk and white
petal of my mother's youth.
From her ear-rings three diamonds

splash a handful of needles,
and I see my mother run back
from rain to the crying cradles.
The rains tack and sew

with broken thread the rags
of the tree-tasselled light.
But her hands are a wet eagle's
two black pink-crinkled feet,

one talon crippled in a garden-
trap set for a mouse. Her saris

do not cling: they hang, loose
feather of a onetime wing.

My cold parchment tongue licks bark
in the mouth when I see her four
still sensible fingers slowly flex
to pick a grain of rice from the kitchen floor.

LOVE POEM FOR A WIFE 1

Really what keeps us apart
at the end of years is unshared
childhood. You cannot, for instance,
meet my father. He is some years
dead. Neither can I meet yours:
he has lately lost his temper
and mellowed.

In the transverse midnight gossip
of cousins' reunions among
brandy fumes, cashews and the Absences
of grandparents, you suddenly grow
nostalgic for my past and I
envy you your village dog-ride
and the mythology

of the seven crazy aunts.
You begin to recognize me
as I pass from ghost to real
and back again in the albums
of family rumours, in brothers'
anecdotes of how noisily
father bathed,

slapping soap on his back;
find sources for a familiar
sheep-mouth look in a sepia wedding
picture of father in a turban,

mother standing on her bare
splayed feet, silver rings
on her second toes;

and reduce the entire career
of my recent unique self
to the compulsion of some high
sentence in His Smilesian diary.
And your father, gone irrevocable
in age, after changing every day
your youth's evenings,

he will acknowledge the wickedness
of no reminiscence: no, not
the burning end of the cigarette
in the balcony, pacing
to and fro as you came to the gate,
late, after what you thought
was an innocent

date with a nice Muslim friend
who only hinted at touches.
Only two weeks ago, in Chicago,
you and brother James started
one of your old drag-out fights
about where the bathroom was
in the backyard,

north or south of the well
next to the jackfruit tree
in your father's father's house
in Alleppey. Sister-in-law
and I were blank cut-outs
fitted to our respective
slots in a room

really nowhere as the two of you
got down to the floor to draw
blueprints of a house from memory
of everything, from newspapers

to the backs of envelopes
and road-maps of the United States
that happened

to flap in the other room
in a midnight wind: you wagered heirlooms
and husband's earnings on what
the Uncle in Kuwait
would say about the Bathroom
and the Well, and the dying,
by now dead,

tree next to it. Probably
only the Egyptians had it right:
their kings had sisters for queens
to continue the incests
of childhood into marriage.
Or we should do as well-meaning
Hindus did,

betroth us before birth,
forestalling separate horoscopes
and mothers' first periods,
and wed us in the oral cradle
and carry marriage back into
the namelessness of childhoods.

SMALL-SCALE REFLECTIONS
ON A GREAT HOUSE

Sometimes I think that nothing
that ever comes into this house
goes out. Things come in every day

to lose themselves among other things
lost long ago among
other things lost long ago;

lame wandering cows from nowhere
have been known to be tethered,
given a name, encouraged

to get pregnant in the broad daylight
of the street under the elders'
supervision, the girls hiding

behind windows with holes in them.

Unread library books
usually mature in two weeks
and begin to lay a row

of little eggs in the ledgers
for fines, as silverfish
in the old man's office room

breed dynasties among long legal words
in the succulence
of Victorian parchment.

Neighbours' dishes brought up
with the greasy sweets they made
all night the day before yesterday

for the wedding anniversary of a god,

never leave the house they enter,
like the servants, the phonographs,
the epilepsies in the blood,

sons-in-law who quite forget
their mothers, but stay to check
accounts or teach arithmetic to nieces,

or the women who come as wives
from houses open on one side
to rising suns, on another

to the setting, accustomed
to wait and to yield to monsoons
in the mountains' calendar

beating through the hanging banana leaves.

And also, anything that goes out
will come back, processed and often
with long bills attached,

like the hooped bales of cotton
shipped off to invisible Manchesters
and brought back milled and folded

for a price, cloth for our days'
middle-class loins, and muslin
for our richer nights. Letters mailed

have a way of finding their way back
with many re-directions to wrong
addresses and red ink marks

earned in Tiruvalla and Sialkot.

And ideas behave like rumours,
once casually mentioned somewhere
they come back to the door as prodigies

born to prodigal fathers, with eyes
that vaguely look like our own,
like what Uncle said the other day:

that every Plotinus we read
is what some Alexander looted
between the malarial rivers.

A beggar once came with a violin
to croak out a prostitute song
that our voiceless cook sang

all the time in our backyard.

Nothing stays out: daughters
get married to short-lived idiots;
sons who run away come back

in grandchildren who recite Sanskrit
to approving old men, or bring
betelnuts for visiting uncles

who keep them gaping with
anecdotes of unseen fathers,
or to bring Ganges water

in a copper pot
for the last of the dying
ancestors' rattle in the throat.

And though many times from everywhere,

recently only twice:
once in nineteen-forty-three
from as far away as the Sahara,

half-gnawed by desert foxes,
and lately from somewhere
in the north, a nephew with stripes

on his shoulder was called
an incident on the border
and was brought back in plane

and train and military truck
even before the telegrams reached,
on a perfectly good

chatty afternoon.

OBITUARY

Father, when he passed on,
left dust
on a table full of papers,
left debts and daughters,
a bedwetting grandson
named by the toss
of a coin after him,

a house that leaned
slowly through our growing
years on a bent coconut
tree in the yard.
Being the burning type,
he burned properly
at the cremation

as before, easily
and at both ends,
left his eye coins
in the ashes that didn't
look one bit different,
several spinal discs, rough,
some burned to coal, for sons

to pick gingerly
and throw as the priest
said, facing east
where three rivers met
near the railway station;
no longstanding headstone
with his full name and two dates

to hold in their parentheses
everything he didn't quite
manage to do himself,
like his caesarian birth
in a brahmin ghetto

and his death by heart-
failure in the fruit market.

But someone told me
he got two lines
in an inside column
of a Madras newspaper
sold by the kilo
exactly four weeks later
to streethawkers

who sell it in turn
to the small groceries
where I buy salt,
coriander,
and jaggery
in newspaper cones
that I usually read

for fun, and lately
in the hope of finding
these obituary lines.
And he left us
a changed mother
and more than
one annual ritual.

Select Reading List

Alphonso-Karkala, John B. *Indo-English Literature in the Nineteenth Century*. Mysore: The Literary Half-yearly, 1970. 34–66, 103–38

Doctor, Geeta. 'The Parsi Quartet' (Keki N. Daruwalla, K. D. Katrak, Gieve Patel, Adil Jussawalla), *Parsiana* (Bombay), April–May 1974. 14–21

Hess, Linda. 'Post-Independence Indian Poetry in English', *Quest* (Bombay), No. 49, January–March 1966. 28–38

Iredale, Roger. 'Indian Poetry in English Today', *Quest* (Bombay), No. 98, November–December 1975. 72–4

Journal of South-Asian Literature, The. Special number on Nissim Ezekiel. Michigan: Oakland University, Fall 1975

Jussawalla, Adil. 'The New Poetry', *Readings in Commonwealth Literature*, ed. William Walsh. Oxford: The Clarendon Press, 1973. 75–90

Karnani, Chetan. *Nissim Ezekiel*. New Delhi: Arnold–Heinemann, 1974

Kohli, Devindra. *Kamala Das*. New Delhi: Arnold–Heinemann, 1975

Kohli, Suresh. 'Interview with Nissim Ezekiel', *Mahfil* (East Lansing, Michigan), Vol. 8, No. 4, Winter 1972. 7–10

Misra, Soubhagya. 'Ezekiel: An Estimation', *graybook* (Cuttack), Vol. 1, No. 1, Spring 1972. 18–27

Padhi, Bibhu Prasad. 'The Parallel Voice: A Study of the New English Poetry in India', *Quest* (Bombay), No. 98, November–December 1975. 39–46

Parthasarathy, R. 'Poet in Search of a Language', *Association of Commonwealth Literature and Language Studies Bulletin* (Mysore), Fourth Series, No. 2, 1975. 9–11

Parthasarathy, R. 'Whoring after English Gods', *Perspectives*, ed. S. P. Bhagwat. Bombay: Popular Prakshan, 1970. 43–60

Peeradina, Saleem, ed. *Contemporary Indian Poetry in English: An Assessment and Selection*. Bombay: Macmillan, 1972

Sergeant, Howard, ed. *Pergamon Poets 9: Poetry from India* (Nissim Ezekiel, A. K. Ramanujan, R. Parthasarathy, Deb Kumar Das). Oxford: Pergamon Press, 1970

Singh, Satyanarain. 'Ramanujan and Ezekiel', *Osmania Journal of English Studies* (Hyderabad), Vol. 7, No. 1, 1969. 67–75

Sivaram Krishna, M. 'Contemporary Indian Poetry in English: An Approach', *Opinion Literary Quarterly* (Bombay), Vol. 1, No. 4, July 1974. 39–57

Taranath, Rajeev and Belliappa, Meena. *The Poetry of Nissim Ezekiel.* Calcutta: Writers Workshop, 1966

Verghese, C. Paul. *Problems of the Indian Creative Writer in English.* Bombay: Somaiya Publications, 1971. 28–45, 55–97

Walsh, William. 'Introduction', *Readings in Commonwealth Literature.* Oxford: Clarendon Press, 1973. xviii–xx

Walsh, William. 'Two Indian Poets' (Nissim Ezekiel, R. Parthasarathy), *The Literary Criterion* (Mysore), Vol. 11, No. 3, Winter 1974. 1–16

Index of Titles

Index of First Lines